The Media Literacy Movement

More and more educators and parents are recognizing the importance of teaching our young people about the media, its messages, and its methods. In New Mexico, for example, all schoolchildren are now required to study media literacy. Similar programs designed to foster media awareness in children are being developed in over a dozen other states. Courses in media literacy are appearing in schools across the nation.

There are many reasons why support for the media literacy movement is growing. Children are spending countless hours watching television and movies; bombarded by images of distorted reality and countless acts of graphic sex and violence. Radio and televsion talk shows flood listeners and viewers with a confusing mix of good and bad advice, sometimes combined with self-serving sales messages. Sensational stories in newspapers and magazines draw readers' attention away from more significant news events. Advertisers employ an arsenal of psychological techniques as they relentlessly try to sell their products in all of the media. Even users of computer-based media are already feeling the pressure of sales pitches and marketing scams.

The media literacy movement is intended to help young people become media-wise. Media-wise readers, viewers, and listeners are equipped to cope with the power of the media. They recognize such basic truths about the media as these:

- The media entertain and teach us, but they can also mislead us.
- Although the media try to be fair, they do not always treat all people equally.
- The media may show the truth, but they may also create false images.
- We can learn about almost any subject from the media, but sometimes the media blur the line between advice, information, and advertisement.
- As the media inform us, they may also try to persuade us.
- Advertisers use various methods to sell their products and may influence us without our knowledge.

Media Today has been created to encourage students not to be passive victims of media power, but rather to become active thinkers who ask questions and seek answers.

Media Literacy and Critical Thinking

A media-wise person is a critical thinker. Indeed, critical thinking skills are an essential part of media literacy. Critical thinking allows readers, viewers, and listeners to distinguish between content and commercialism, to recognize bias and distortion, and to better understand the role of the media in our society.

Theorists offer various definitions of critical thinking. These definitions share several common features. Critical thinkers are able and willing to examine diverse viewpoints about an issue, despite any possible vested interest they may have. They use facts and reasons to support or refute arguments. Critical thinkers try to think for themselves, instead of simply accepting ideas that have been passed down to them. Critical thinkers also think about the process of thinking itself, always striving for greater clarity, accuracy, insight, and fairness in their thinking.

One important theorist on critical thinking is Benjamin Bloom. He identifies six broad categories of thinking skills in a hierarchy, from

lowest order to highest order. These skills are: knowing, comprehending, applying, analyzing, synthesizing, and evaluating. "Knowing", the lowest level, is simple recall or identification. "Evaluating" is the highest level, synonymous with critical thinking itself. Evaluating requires the application of the other skills in the hierarchy. Critical thinking, therefore, is both a set of skills and a process involving the interaction of these skills.

Another important theorist on critical thinking is Richard Paul, director of the Center for Critical Thinking and Moral Critique, at Sonoma State University. Paul describes a critical thinker as one who evaluates reasons and brings thought and action in line with these evaluations. Paul says that critical thinkers analyze and evaluate reasons and evidence; make assumptions explicit and evaluate them; reject unwarranted inferences, or "leaps of logic"; use the best and most complete evidence available; make relevant distinctions; clarify; avoid inconsistency and contradiction; reconcile apparent contradictions; and distinguish what they know from what they merely suspect to be true. Paul and his colleagues developed a list of critical thinking strategies. Many of the critical thinking skills that underlie the lessons of *Media Today* are based on these strategies.

Incorporating Media Workshop into Your Curriculum

Media Today provides engaging, relevant, and up-to-date learning materials designed to develop and apply students' skills as media-wise critical thinkers. The lessons and activities provide opportunities for:

- reading and writing
- discussing and debating issues and ideas

- evaluating the credibility and intent of sources
- analyzing, evaluating, and interpreting ideas and information
- recognizing hidden messages
- exploring assumptions and implications
- forming and expressing opinions
- drawing conclusions.

Media Today can be effectively used in any of various subject areas, including language arts, English, social studies, journalism, and communications. The materials are suitable for both independent use and cooperative learning.

The Elements of Media Workshop

Media Today is a consumable worktext that provides a variety of learning materials and application activities. The book begins with a three-page opening section, "The Power of the Media", that presents an overview of the book's themes and introduces the concept of media literacy. *Media Today* is then divided into four parts. Part 1 focuses on newspapers and magazines. Part 2 deals with audio media: radio and recordings. Part 3 examines television and the movies, and Part 4 explores computer-based media.

Each part of the student book opens with a two-page introduction followed by two or three units. Each unit consists of text, several lessons, media-related sidenotes, discussion prompts, a unit activity, and an end-of-unit evaluation. In addition, each of the book's four parts also contains a two-page feature about advertising and a concluding project. A glossary appears at the end of the book.

The part opener introduces students to the specific media that are the focus of the units

that follow. The unit text provides information about the media and explores significant ideas and issues. Unit texts vary in their manner of presentation. In addition to reading expository text, students read a play, "listen to" a talk show, sit in on a programming session, and read a portion of a fictional magazine.

The lessons engage students in reading, writing, speaking, and listening. The lessons blend instruction in media methods with opportunities to use critical thinking skills, both inside and outside the classroom. Sidenotes in the unit texts and the lessons provide instruction, emphasize important information, and raise key questions.

The end-of-unit activities let students follow through and build on what they have learned. The unit evaluations test students' understanding of the lessons and also provide questions for self-evaluation. The project at the end of each part allows students to synthesize information and apply their media knowledge and critical thinking skills in a final product or presentation.

Media Today is appropriate for students of all ability levels and learning styles. The *Teacher's Resource Manual* offers teaching suggestions and procedures for helping students develop and improve both their media awareness and their critical thinking skills.

PRACTICAL SUGGESTIONS

The suggestions that follow are provided to help you achieve maximum benefit from using *Media Today* with diverse student populations.

Managing Cooperative Learning

In cooperative learning, students work together in groups of three to six. Many of the activities in *Media Today* are designed for use by cooperative groups. Use the following suggestions to manage cooperative group activities in your classroom:

- Create a positive atmosphere for the idea of cooperative groups by explaining that students will work together, share ideas, and help one another.
- Make sure groups include students of varying ability levels. Such diversity fosters discussion, peer teaching, and the use of higher-order thinking skills.
- Have students sit in a circle for greater face-to-face interaction.
- Post or provide photocopies of general behavior guidelines, such as the following: remain in your group, respect others, speak softly, do not criticize, do not interrupt, and do not make personal attacks.
- Explain the goal or objective for the group. You may want to write the objective on the chalkboard or hand out photocopied sheets showing the objective.
- Assign specific roles for each group member, such as summarizer, facilitator, note-taker, and timekeeper. Make sure that roles and responsibilities are clear, both individually and in relation to the group objective.
- Monitor each group's activities. A good strategy is to sit with students. Ask questions, model tasks, redirect efforts, and restate goals, as necessary.
- Create a formal observation sheet to help you evaluate each student and each group. Award points for active listening, asking relevant questions, contributing ideas, and encouraging others.
- Rotate students through several groups throughout the year. This process avoids

boredom and allows students to work with a greater number of classmates.

- Allow time for students to discuss, summarize, and evaluate their group experience. Propose that students answer such questions as these:

What problems did we have?
How did we overcome them?
How did each task help us reach the goal?
How could we have improved our work?

- Give students both individual and group grades. This will increase students' accountability within the group.

Teaching ESL/LEP Students

Strategies for teaching ESL/LEP students are included in the teaching suggestions for each of the four parts of *Media Today* (pages 2-62). In addition, the following suggestions will be helpful:

- Write all assignments on the chalkboard, in addition to giving instructions orally.
- Because ESL/LEP students can have trouble interpreting directions, give examples of what you expect.
- Explain or model specific strategies for students, indicating how the strategies help students learn.
- Ask students to explain tasks and to describe how they carried out those tasks.
- Draw on students' personal interests and prior knowledge when introducing new topics, concepts, or skills.
- Provide multiple ways for students to become involved in the learning process. See "Accommodating Diverse Learning Styles" on this page.
- Provide a brief, clear overview of a topic before students begin to study it.

- Model and clarify important vocabulary.
- Model critical thinking skills by using simple examples.
- Encourage students to ask questions.
- Pair students with a native speaker of English for specific tasks.
- Include students in cooperative learning groups.
- Use graphic organizers to help students recognize categories and relationships.
- Encourage students to use these devices to generate and clarify ideas.
- Provide additional resources, such as books, articles, pictures, and videos.
- Repeat, paraphrase, or simplify language to help students understand ideas and information.

Accommodating Diverse Learning Styles

Students learn and think in different ways. Although most students receive information through their five senses, each student tends to prefer to learn through one sense, such as the visual or auditory modality. A student's preference for a certain sensory modality is that student's learning style—the mental patterns that shape the way the student perceives, remembers, and thinks.

There are three main learning styles. Visual learners learn best by seeing information. Auditory learners learn best by hearing information. Kinesthetic or tactile learners learn best by moving about and using their hands to feel and manipulate objects.

Students also tend to prefer one of two kinds of thinking styles—global or analytical. Global thinkers are deductive, preferring an overall picture first, from which they analyze and incorporate details. Analytical thinkers are

inductive, preferring first to analyze details and then to form the larger picture. Some students prefer one style to another in given situations; others prefer one style regardless of the situation.

In tailoring instruction and materials for your students, keep in mind a student's learning style and thinking style. You will find that the lessons and activities in *Media Today* address a variety of learning and thinking styles. The following suggestions will help you meet your student's needs.

Visual Learners

- Display vocabulary on the board, on a poster, or on an overhead transparency. Provide visual clues to meaning, such as photographs and context clues.
- Provide supplementary visual materials for texts and lessons, such as photographs, drawings, videotapes, and CD-ROMs.
- Demonstrate or model tasks, concepts, and relationships.
- Write instructions on the chalkboard, accompanied by appropriate examples.
- Use graphic organizers, and encourage students to use them.

Auditory Learners

- Ask volunteers to read texts aloud or to make audio recordings that auditory learners can listen to.
- Read instructions aloud and repeat them as needed. Record instructions so that students can listen to repeated playbacks.
- Allow time for class and group discussion.

Kinesthetic or Tactile Learners

- Encourage students to take notes. Physical hand movements help these students learn and remember new information.
- Encourage students to draw, make diagrams, and use graphic organizers.
- Provide content-related objects for students to handle.
- Involve students in role-playing.
- Set up field trips that relate to the content or thinking skills covered.

Global Thinkers

- Provide an overview of a topic, concept, or skill when introducing it to students.
- Encourage the use of imagination and mental imagery to help students understand new topics, concepts, or skills.
- Explore ways that ideas and information are relevant to students' lives.

Analytical Thinkers

- Introduce new material by first identifying key details, facts, or examples. Then present an overview.
- Encourage students to set goals and to assess their performance in meeting them.
- Allow time for students to take an organized, step-by-step approach to their work.
- Help students recognize how topics, ideas, and skills relate to their lives.

THE POWER OF THE MEDIA

The opening pages of *Media Today* introduce students to the concept of media literacy and touch on several key points. These points are developed throughout the book. They include the following:

- Mass media communicate with huge numbers of people.

- The media can serve different purposes. They can inform, entertain, or persuade.

- The media are powerful because they influence the way people think and act.

- Media-wise readers, viewers, and listeners do not simply accept what they see and hear.

- Advertising and the media are intertwined.

Have students read pages 1-4 either independently or aloud, section by section. Discuss each section, asking students to summarize the main ideas. The following suggestions will help you focus the discussion.

- Write important terms on the chalkboard, and discuss their meaning. Include: mass communication, media (and medium), mass media, media-wise, media literacy.

- Direct students' attention to the illustrations on page 1. Have students discuss each illustration.

- On the chalkboard, write the eight kinds of mass media listed on page 2. Encourage students to talk about their experiences with each medium and their personal likes and dislikes.

- Discuss the media literacy ideas listed on page 1. Ask students to give examples from their own experience. Stress that these are some of the underlying ideas of *Media Today*.

FOCUS ON NEWSPAPERS AND MAGAZINES

INTRODUCTION TO PART 1 (PAGES 1-3)

Getting Started

Begin discussion by asking students why they think people read newspapers and magazines. Then ask students which newspapers and magazines they read. List the responses on the chalkboard. Take a survey to find out which papers and magazines are read by the greatest number of students. Discuss why these papers and magazines are popular.

Reading the Text

Have students read the introduction to Part 1, pages 1-3. You may want to direct students to pause after each section to discuss such key questions as these:

Readers and Topics

- What is meant by the statement, "Newspapers and magazines offer something for everyone."?
- The author writes that newspapers and magazines are "portable". What does this mean? Are televisions and radios portable in the same sense?

Advertising

- "It pays to advertise" is an old saying. What does this saying mean?
- Why are advertisements so important to newspaper and magazine publishers?

Impact

- Nearly every home in the United States has at least one television set. Why do newspapers and magazines nevertheless serve as key sources of information?
- What is meant by the statement, "Newspapers and magazines shape people's opinions."?

Issues

- Do you agree or disagree with each of the criticisms mentioned? Why?
- Should there be limits on what newspapers and magazines can print? If so, who should set these limits?

SPECIAL STRATEGIES AND ACTIVITIES

Teaching suggestions for each section of Part 1 of the worktext are provided in the pages that follow. The specific suggestions below will assist you in teaching ESL/LEP students, in linking the material with language arts and social studies curricula, and in using cooperative learning.

ESL/LEP Strategies

- The KWL technique—Know, Want to Know, and Learned—is useful for helping students comprehend new material. Create a chart with the three headings. Ask students what they already know about a particular topic—newspapers, for example. Write their ideas in the first column. Then ask what they would like to know. List students' responses in the second column. After students read the text, ask them to summarize the main points they have learned. Record their responses in the third column of the chart.

- The sidenotes contain a great deal of useful information. You may want to pair ESL/LEP students with more proficient readers who can read the information aloud and discuss key points. Encourage ESL/LEP students to ask questions about information and specific words or terms they do not understand.
- Students whose native language is not English may benefit from examining newspapers and magazines written in the language they are most familiar with. Students can also compare English-language newspapers and magazines with non-English publications.

Language Arts Links

- Newspapers and magazines offer almost unlimited opportunities for integrating media-related content into the language arts curriculum. Students might, for example, analyze sentence and paragraph structure, examine articles for the use of quotations and dialogue, or compare writers' use of descriptive and narrative techniques.
- Encourage students to try their hand at writing the different kinds of articles they encounter. Then discuss which articles were easiest to write, which were most difficult, and why.
- Explore with students how writers use language to create desired effects and send hidden messages. In Unit1, Lesson 1, for example, students consider the connotation of words in headlines as they consider implied judgments. Have students analyze and discuss newspaper and magazine articles as well as print advertisements.

Social Studies Links

- Use newspapers and news magazines to explore current events and world issues. Discuss questions such as these: Which topics receive the most coverage? Which parts of the world get the most attention? What kinds of events are considered "news"?
- Examine the role of the print media in political campaigns and elections. Discuss questions such as these: How do newspapers and magazines help to create a candidate's image? Do newspapers and magazines do an adequate job of informing voters? Do journalists go too far in investigating candidates' personal lives?
- Discuss the statement, "Today's news is tomorrow's history." How true is it? Do all news events become part of history, or are some simply forgotten? How much of the content of social studies textbooks previously appeared in newspapers? Which of today's news events *should* be covered in future social studies books?

Cooperative Learning

In addition to the various cooperative learning activities and projects in the worktext, Part 1 offers many other opportunities for cooperative learning. Here are a few suggestions.

- Have students work together in small groups to create the front page of a newspaper. Students should write the articles, plan the layout, and create the headlines.
- Have student groups create and carry out a survey of readers' habits. Students might research what newspapers and magazines friends and relatives read, when they do their reading, which kinds of articles are

favorites, and so on. Groups can then share and compare their survey results.

- Have students work in groups to develop plans for a special interest magazine. Students should discuss what the subject matter will be and who the target audience is. Then students can plan the specific content of an issue and suggest likely advertisers.

UNIT 1

NEWSPAPERS: BRINGING YOU THE EVENTS OF THE DAY (PAGES 6-8)

Getting Started

Explain that Unit 1 deals with newspapers. Direct students' attention to the clippings displayed on pages 4-5. Discuss the wide variety of clippings shown. Point out that newspapers are published not only in cities and towns across the United States but also in countries around the world. Indeed, newspapers are written in countless languages. You may want to ask students what non-English newspapers they may have seen.

Teaching Suggestions

Have students read Unit 1, "Newspapers: Bringing You the Events of the Day", pages 6-10. Use the following suggestions to highlight important points and reinforce content.

What News Do Papers Cover?

- List key terms on the chalkboard, including *international news, national news, regional news,* and *local news.* Have students explain, in their own words, the

differences between these various kinds of news. Ask students to give examples of each kind of news.
- To extend the discussion, have students find articles in a daily newspaper that exemplify each kind of news.

Kinds of Newspapers

- Display examples of different kinds of papers, including mainstream (traditional) as well as tabloid newspapers. (Note: Lesson 2 of this unit will introduce students to the terms *mainstream* (or *traditional*) *newspaper* and *tabloid.*) Have students identify similarities and differences in the appearance of the papers. For example, direct students to compare the size and number of headlines and photos.
- Stress the point made in the sidenote that publishers include articles that appeal to specific groups of readers. Emphasize that advertisers will want to buy ad space in the paper in order to reach particular readers.

Who Publishes the News?

- List on the chalkboard examples of the kinds of workers who put together a newspaper. Ask students to explain how publishing a newspaper is a team effort.
- As an extension activity, have a member of the school newspaper visit the class. Discuss how news for the paper is gathered and published.

Newspapers and Advertising

- Most students will probably be surprised to learn just how important advertising is to a newspaper's survival. Spend some time discussing the significance of this point. Note the power that advertisers

have. Suppose, for example, that an airline said that it did not want its advertisement to appear near any stories about plane crashes. Would the newspaper comply with the airline's request? Why?

- Have students examine a newspaper and estimate the ratio of ad pages to news pages.
- Discuss which advertisements appear within the body of a newspaper and which are placed in separate sections. Explain the advantages of grouping similar kinds of advertisements together, such as employment ads and automobile ads.

Lesson 1

HARD NEWS AND SOFT NEWS (PAGES 9-10)

Objective: Students use critical thinking skills to analyze newspaper articles.

Getting Started

Ask students for examples of recent news stories. List examples on the chalkboard. Discuss how these stories are alike and how they differ. Ask questions such as these:

- Which stories focus on people? Which focus on places? Which focus on events?
- Which stories are most important? Which are least important?
- Which stories are the easiest to understand? Why? Which are the most difficult? Why?

Teaching Suggestions

Have students read "Lesson 1: Hard News and Soft News", pages 9-10. Use the following suggestions to highlight important points and reinforce content.

- Ask students to imagine the results if newspapers did not group related content into sections. Suppose, for example, that each page contained a mixture of news, sports, and entertainment articles. Ask whether this would help or hinder readers, and why.
- Have students describe how hard news differs from soft news. Then ask them why they think most papers contain more soft news than hard news. Discuss which kind of news is generally more important, and why. Use the examples listed on page 8 for discussion purposes. You may also want to have students provide additional examples.
- Have students summarize, in their own words, the difference between a *fact* and an *opinion*. Ask why it is important to distinguish one from the other when reading a newspaper.
- Direct students' attention to "The Language of Thinking" sidenote on page 9. After comparing the two headlines, extend the discussion by examining other examples of how writers can choose words to create a desired effect. One way to do this is to have students compare the connotation of each of a pair of words, such as *careful/fussy, slender/skinny, statesman/politician, dog/mutt.*
- Have students answer questions 1-4 on pages 9-10. You may want to have some students work in pairs or small groups to discuss the articles and answer the questions.

Answers to Questions on Pages 9-10

Students' answers will vary depending on the articles chosen. Use the following guidelines to help you evaluate students' responses.

1. Students should identify the most important ideas of each article.
2. Students should distinguish between facts and opinions and provide specific examples from the articles. (Refer back to the sidenote on page 9 for definitions of *fact* and *opinion*.)
3. Students should recognize judgments, whether made or implied. (Refer back to the sidenote on page 10 for a definition of *imply*.)
4. Students should recognize various purposes. Some students may point out that an article can serve more than one purpose.

Lesson 2

FACTS OR FEELINGS? (PAGES 11-13)

Objective: Students analyze and compare articles from mainstream and tabloid newspapers.

Getting Started

Display the front page of a serious, mainstream newspaper and the front page of a tabloid. Discuss with students what feeling each page conveys and how it conveys that feeling. Ask students which paper they would be more likely to pick up and read, and why.

Teaching Suggestions

Have students read "Lesson 2: Facts or Feelings?", pages 11-13. Use the following suggestions to highlight important points and reinforce content.

- Use the chalkboard to compare the features of newspapers. Make two lists, using the headings *Mainstream Newspapers* and *Tabloid Newspapers*. Have students suggest key features for each list.

- Discuss with students what is meant by the claim that "tabloid news makes readers feel instead of think". Ask them whether or not they agree, and why.
- To help students perceive differences between the two articles on page 12, read them aloud to the class.
- Discuss "The Language of Thinking" sidenote on page 12. Then have students answer questions 1-6 on pages 12-13.
- For the "Discussion" on page 13, tell students to support their opinions with specific reasons. Encourage students to listen carefully to viewpoints that differ from their own.
- Using the sidenote on page 13 as a jumping-off point, you may want to have a class discussion or debate about censorship.

Answers to Questions on Pages 12-13

1. Christopher Reeve was seriously injured in a fall from a horse during a riding competition. He is a 42-year-old actor.
2. Students should recognize that the tabloid article is less formal and more sensational than the mainstream article.
3. Students should recognize that the mainstream article simply reports what happened and how it happened. The tabloid article builds in drama by describing the fall and the resulting injury.
4. The drama of the tabloid is meant to make readers feel. For example, the tabloid quotes the nurse's emotional words.
5. The mainstream headline is low-key. The tabloid is much more dramatic.
6. The mainstream article immediately takes a factual approach. The tabloid "hooks" the reader by referring to Superman.

Lesson 3

ARTICLES THAT TRY TO PERSUADE (PAGES 14-15)

Objective: Students analyze and evaluate an editorial and explore opposing viewpoints.

Getting Started

Have students read and discuss several letters to the editor in a newspaper. Ask students why people write such letters and why people like to read them. Explain that newspapers contain both facts and opinions. Stress that critical readers look for opinions to be supported by facts.

Teaching Suggestions

Have students read "Lesson 3: Articles That Try to Persuade", pages 14-15. Use the following suggestions to highlight important points and reinforce content.

- Stress that editorials and columns can help readers understand issues, but that readers must also weigh opposing viewpoints before forming their own opinions.
- Have students examine an op-ed page and identify columns, articles, and other items. Discuss the question posed in the sidenote on page 14: "How can reading both the editorial page and the op-ed page give you a balanced view of issues?"
- Discuss the various methods writers use to persuade readers. Elicit examples of these methods from students. Ask which of these methods politicians use.
- Read the editorial on page 14 aloud to the class to help students perceive the feeling behind the words.

- Discuss "The Language of Thinking" sidenote on page 15. Then have students answer questions 1-7 on pages 15.

Answers to Questions on Page 15

1. "People pollution" is ruining the Grand Canyon and other national parks.
2. Nearly 5 million people visited the Grand Canyon in 1994. The summer of 1995, more than 25,000 people visited the park daily. Visitors leave garbage and cause noise.
3. The writer wants to limit the number of visitors, ban motor vehicles and planes, impose fines on people who litter, and hire more rangers.
4. A news article would focus on facts rather than take an outright stand on the issue.
5. The writer wants to alarm people and create a sense of destruction.
6. One possible opposing argument is that national parks must be open to visitors at the time of year when most can come, which is generally summer.
7. Students should recognize that although the writer supports a viewpoint with facts, it is still only one viewpoint.

Unit Activity
COMPARING NEWSPAPERS (PAGE 16)

- In this cooperative-learning activity, student groups examine and compare two newspapers. Before students begin, you may want to review key terms, such as *international* and *national news, hard* and *soft news, mainstream* and *tabloid.*
- Follow up the activity by having groups compare their answers to the final question. What conclusions about student preferences can the class as a whole draw?

7

Unit Evaluation
(PAGE 17)

Possible responses to the questions follow.

Checking What You Learned:

1. Students should agree. Distinguishing between fact and opinion is an essential part of critical reading.
2. The second statement is true. The first statement may be true sometimes, but not always.
3. Readers should recognize when the writer of an article is trying to influence them. Understanding an article's purpose also aids comprehension.
4. Reading several editorials and columns about the same issue will help the reader see different sides of the issue and enable the reader to make a well-informed judgment.

Checking How You Learned:

Have students share and compare their answers. Encourage students to support their ideas with facts and examples.

UNIT 2

MAGAZINES: FACTS, VIEWS, AND FUN (PAGES 18-29)

Getting Started

Explain that Unit 2 deals with magazines. Ask students to think about interesting or entertaining magazines they have read. Have students identify magazine elements they like, such as action photos or gossipy interviews. Ask students to describe similarities and differences between magazines and newspapers. Then discuss what it is magazines offer that other forms of media (such as television and radio) do not.

Teaching Suggestions

Have students read "Unit 2, Magazines: Facts, Views, and Fun", pages 18-20. Use the following suggestions to highlight important points and reinforce content.

- Be sure students understand the difference between general interest magazines and special interest magazines. If possible, bring in some samples of both types of magazines for students to examine.
- You may want to share with students a copy of *Writer's Market*. This book, which describes and categorizes magazines of all kinds, is updated each year. You can find it in most libraries and bookstores. Students will be amazed at just how specific audiences can be for special-interest magazines.
- Discuss the questions posed in the sidenote on page 19: "Would you advertise in a general or a special-interest magazine? Why?"

Why People Read Magazines

- Discuss this statement on page 19: "Magazines . . . let readers share other people's experience and knowledge." Ask students *how* magazines do this. Point out that some magazine articles are written in the first person (*I*), some in the second person (*you*), and some in the third person (*he, she, they*).
- When discussing editorials and columns in magazines, refer back to Lesson 3 of Unit 1: "Articles that Persuade," on page 14. Review the definition of *editorial* and *column,* and discuss why people write and read such articles.

- Have students examine sample magazines to see the range of articles that publishers mix together. Also, discuss the mixture of advertisements. Ask students if they can tell from studying the contents of a magazine who reads the magazine.

Who Writes Magazine Articles?

- Discuss with students how writers do research. Point out that they may use a variety of information sources, such as books, newspapers, magazines, computer resources, and interviews. Ask students which of these sources they have used in researching papers and projects for school. Discuss the importance of accurate, careful research. Ask what the consequences might be if a magazine writer did faulty or incomplete research.
- Call students' attention to the sidenote on page 20. Discuss how knowing the qualifications of the writer, "will help you judge the article's content". Point out that sometimes a well-researched article by a non-expert can have more value than an article written by a so-called expert. Stress that students should not blindly accept a single "expert opinion", because experts frequently disagree with one another.

The Power of Magazines

- Explore with students how articles achieve "a friendly informal tone". (Refer back to the sidenote in Unit 1, Lesson 2, page 12 to review the definition of *tone*.) Share some article excerpts with the class in which the "writer seems to talk directly to you".
- Ask students to give examples of how magazines let readers know what's "hot" and what's not.
- As an extension activity, have students go to the library and observe how various magazine covers are designed to get readers' attention. (Students may work individually or in small groups.) Have students share and compare their observations.

Lesson 1

PLANNING THE ARTICLES (PAGES 21-22)

Objective: Students analyze a magazine article and explore its link with advertising.

Getting Started

Share with students copies of two very different magazines, such as *Money* and *Seventeen*. Ask what the magazines have in common (for example, they both contain various kinds of articles and advertisements). Then ask how the magazines differ, and why. Guide students toward the idea that each magazine's content is tailored to a particular audience. Extend the discussion by having students suggest readers who might read both magazines.

Teaching Suggestions

Have students read "Lesson 1: Planning the Articles", pages 21-22. Use the following suggestions to highlight important points and reinforce content.

- Expand the discussion of "time of year" by having students suggest possible articles for different seasons for various magazines. For instance, what articles might be appropriate for a summer issue of *TV Guide*? A spring issue of *YM*? A winter issue of *Sports Illustrated*? Encourage students to explain the reasons behind their suggestions. You

may want to have students suggest possible advertisements as well.

- Direct students' attention to the first sidenote on page 21. Point out that, like *democracy*, the word *demographics* comes from Greek *demos*, meaning "the people". Stress that demographics is an important consideration for all media. Discuss the questions posed in the sidenote: "How can demographics help a magazine publisher? Why is demographics important to advertisers?"

- Direct students' attention to the second sidenote on page 21. Discuss ways in which advertising money gives power to advertisers and enables them to influence magazine content. For example, advertisers do not want any articles that cast their products in a negative light, either directly or indirectly. Thus, the maker of a sugary breakfast cereal would not be happy with an article discussing the bad effects of sugar. On the other hand, the cereal maker would encourage the magazine to mention cereal in articles relating to eating breakfast or shopping for food.

- In discussing the article excerpt on page 21, point out techniques that the writer uses to engage the reader. For instance, the writer begins by asking the reader two questions. Also, the writer is writing in the second person (*you*).

- Have students answer questions 1-7 on page 22. You may want to have some students work in pairs or small groups to discuss the article and answer the questions.

- For the "Discussion" on page 22, tell students to support their opinions with specific reasons. Encourage students to listen carefully to viewpoints that differ from their own.

Answers to Questions on Page 22

1. The purpose of the article is to encourage readers to "get up and get skating".
2. The magazine is aimed at teens, who are likely to be interested in trying in-line skating.
3. The article is factual in its description of in-line skates and protective gear. Telling readers that they will "have a blast" is an opinion. The champion's endorsement of a particular brand of skates is also an opinion.
4. Students should recognize that the writer probably got her information from interviewing people and perhaps from personal experience.
5. Students should note that, as mentioned on page 21, *Power-Up!* skates is one of the magazine's advertisers.
6. Again, as mentioned on page 21, *STAR-1* clothing is one of the magazine's advertisers.
7. Students should recognize that the article has linked the two particular brands with a "hot" sports activity. Also a "skating champion" has endorsed the brand of skates.

Lesson 2

LOOKING CLOSELY AT MAGAZINES (PAGES 23-25)

Objective: Students analyze and compare magazines in terms of content and audience.

Getting Started

Explain to students that each year numerous magazines fail, while others do well. Have students brainstorm reasons why some magazines succeed while others do not. Guide them to understand that one of the main

principles of magazine success is to clearly identify an audience and then effectively aim the content of the magazine at that audience.

Teaching Suggestions

Have students read "Lesson 2: Looking Closely at Magazines", pages 23-25. Use the following suggestions to highlight important points and reinforce content.

- Write the phrase *target audience* on the chalkboard. Discuss the meaning of the term, and have students identify the target audience of various magazines. Extend the discussion by asking students to identify the target audience for several television programs, movies, and radio shows. Point out that advertisers have a target in mind when they create ads for the various media.
- You may want to have students work in pairs or small groups to analyze and compare the two magazines. If so, encourage students to share and discuss ideas as they answer questions 1-7 on pages 24-25.
- Discuss "The Language of Thinking" sidenote on page 24. Extend the discussion by exploring with students how other media, such as newspapers and TV shows, also have an image. Take the discussion even further by discussing the images of people, and why such images are important. For example, why is image important to a politician? To an actor? To an employee? To a student? Also ask students how easy or difficult it is for a person to change his or her image.

Answers to Questions on Pages 24-25

Students' answers will vary depending on the magazines chosen. Use the following guidelines to help you evaluate students' responses.

1. Some possible clues are the titles of the articles, the people shown in photos, and the kinds of products advertised.
2. Possible responses include the kinds of articles included, the style of writing, and the use of artwork.
3. Answers will vary. You may want to point out that some ads are for products, while others are for services.
4. Clues to target audience include the language of the ad, the age and sex of the people shown, and the situations depicted.
5. Responses will vary. Students should support their answers with clear reasons.
6. Students should identify similarities in both content and format. Encourage students to be specific.
7. Students should recognize differences in both content and format. You may also want to have students identify differences in tone and use of language.

Lesson 3

LOOKING BEYOND THE WORDS (PAGES 26-27)

Objective: Students use critical thinking skills to analyze a magazine article.

Getting Started

Discuss with students various ways that writers communicate their personal feelings through their writing. For example, writers may state their opinions outright or imply them. They may omit certain information or stress only one side of an argument. They may use positively or negatively charged words (for instance, a large group of people may be a "crowd" or a "mob"). Point out that it may be all but impossible for anyone to

write a totally objective article, since every decision that a writer makes—what facts to include, what language to use—reflects his or her viewpoint.

Teaching Suggestions

Have students read "Lesson 3: Looking Beyond the Words", pages 26-27. Use the following suggestions to highlight important points and reinforce content.

- Ask students what an *assumption* is. Guide them to understand that an assumption is something assumed or taken for granted—that is, accepted as a fact. Explain that we all make assumptions. Elicit or provide some examples.

- Point out that writers and speakers often make assumptions. Explain that critical readers watch for assumptions and question whether they are true. As an example, call students' attention to the doctor's statement in the article on page 26: "Teens don't see the dangers. They think nothing can hurt them." Elicit or explain that the doctor is making an assumption about all teens. Ask students if they think this assumption is true. You may also want to note that an assumption is often expressed as a *generalization*, as it is here.

- Discuss the title of the article: "Teens Are Risking Their Lives". Ask students how this title reflects the writer's viewpoint. Ask why the writer didn't simply call the article, "The Dangers of Huffing".

- Discuss the sidenote on page 27. Then have students answer questions 1-7 on pages 27.

Answers to Questions on Page 27

1. Huffing is a dangerous practice that is killing or injuring more and more teenagers.

2. The article consists mainly of fact. For example, the writer tells what huffing is, describes the effects and dangers, and cites statistics.

3. The writer stresses the dangers of huffing and uses alarming words like *poison*. Students should also realize that the doctor's words, that the writer has chosen to quote, probably reflect the writer's feelings as well.

4. Teens may think twice before trying such a dangerous practice. Parents may be on guard against huffing, an activity they may not even have heard of before.

5. The article's purpose is to warn readers of the dangers of huffing. Students will probably feel that the writer has accomplished this purpose.

6. Students are likely to object to the implication. Encourage them to support their objections with clear reasons.

7. Students may say that a teen would have used different language and might have said more about the "high" huffers get.

Unit Activity
WRITING FOR A MAGAZINE (PAGE 28)

- In this activity, students write an article for a magazine they like to read. Students work independently or in groups of two or three. Encourage students to spend time brainstorming, planning, and outlining before starting to write. Suggest that students make their topic as specific as possible, because a topic that is too broad will be difficult to cover adequately.

- You can extend the "Follow-Up" suggestion by having students rewrite their articles—or one or two paragraphs of their articles—for different audiences. Discuss the various kinds of changes that are necessary. For example, if an article about a band in a teen magazine were rewritten for an adult magazine, what changes in language might be made? What changes in content?

Unit Evaluation (PAGE 29)

Possible responses to the questions follow.

Checking What You Learned:

1. Students should agree. Most magazines depend on advertising money for their survival. Publishers will generally try to accommodate advertisers to keep them happy.
2. Reading just Article #2 would give you only one point of view, while reading Article #1 would give you a balanced view, better enabling you to form an opinion. Reading both articles would also expose you to more than one viewpoint.
3. Although the special interest magazine has fewer readers, those readers all share a definite interest. Another factor to consider is that ads probably cost less in the special-interest magazine.
4. The editor must tailor the content of the magazine to the specific readers.

Checking How You Learned:

Have students share and compare their answers. Encourage students to support their ideas with facts and examples.

ADVERTISING IN THE PRINT MEDIA (PAGES 30-31)

Getting Started

Have students recall advertisements they have seen in newspapers and magazines. Ask which ones they remember best. Why do those ads stand out in their minds?

Teaching Suggestions

Have students read the feature on advertising in the print media (pages 30-31). You may want to direct students to stop after each section to allow for class discussion. Use the following suggestions to highlight important points and reinforce content.

- As class discussion focuses on each advertising method, ask students for other examples of the method that they have seen. Point out that the same methods are also used in TV and radio commercials.
- Explain that certain advertising methods work especially well with particular audiences. For example, the bandwagon approach is often used with teenage audiences because most teens like to feel that they are part of the crowd. Ask students which advertising methods would be most (or least) effective with various audiences, such as children, teens, adults, senior citizens, men, and women.
- As an additional activity, have students look through newspapers and magazines to find examples of the advertising methods discussed: bandwagon, exaggeration, unique claim, and rhetorical question. You may want to have students work together to create a classroom display.

PROJECT
READING BETWEEN THE LINES
(PAGES 32-35)

- Lead into the project by discussing desirable traits of critical readers. Guide students in creating a list on the chalkboard by having them complete this sentence: "Critical readers should be able to . . ." List such phrases as these: distinguish fact from opinion, understand an author's purpose, recognize implied messages, and so on. Encourage students to refer back to this list as they choose articles and ads and develop their writing tips.

- The following questions may help you evaluate students' performance on the project: Were students able to work together to select a variety of appropriate articles and ads? Were students' tips focused on key aspects of critical reading? Were students' tips expressed clearly and effectively? Did students learn from comparing other groups' booklets with their own?

FOCUS ON AUDIO MEDIA

INTRODUCTION TO PART 2 (PAGES 36-81)

Getting Started

Begin discussion by defining *audio media*. Explain that *audio* means something that can be heard. Ask students to describe media they think fall in this category. List "radio" and "music" on the chalkboard. Ask students why people listen to the radio. List reasons on the chalkboard. Then ask students which stations they listen to and which programs are their favorites and why.

Reading the Text

Have students read the introduction to Part 2 (pages 36-37). You may want to direct students to pause after each section to discuss such key questions as these:

Programming

- What are the two main reasons people listen to radio?
- How are information radio and entertainment radio different?

Audience

- What are some examples of different audiences for different radio programs?
- Which is the most popular kind of radio—FM or AM?
- What are some of the ways people listen to radio?

Funding

- How do most radio stations earn profits?
- How are member stations of National Public Radio different from other stations?
- How do stations decide on the amount to charge advertisers?
- How do recording companies earn profits?

Impact

- What are some of the ways in which radio has had an influence in America?

Issues

- Do you agree with the complaints some people have about radio and the music that is played on radio? Why?
- Do you believe certain kinds of music should be banned or censored? Why?

SPECIAL STRATEGIES AND ACTIVITIES

Teaching suggestions for each section of Part 1 of the worktext are provided in the pages that follow. The specific suggestions below will assist you in teaching ESL/LEP students, in linking the material with language arts and social studies curricula, and in using cooperative learning.

ESL/LEP Strategies

- The emphasis on audio media in this part provides an opportunity for students to use and strengthen listening and oral language skills. Encourage students to listen to radio programs and to discuss questions they have about what they hear.

- The innuendoes and connotations of spoken English may be hard for some students to grasp. Ask non-native English speakers to identify similar strategies in their native languages—ways in which a speaker can say one thing but mean something else.
- Encourage students whose native language is not English to listen to stations in their native language and to compare them with English-language stations.
- The vignettes in this part provide opportunities for role-playing that will benefit students. You may want to have students practice their parts with a native-English speaker.

Language Arts Links

- This part provides an opportunity for students to compare spoken and written language styles. Encourage students to observe how spoken dialogue includes contractions, sentence fragments, sounds, and slurred word combinations such as "uh huh" and "whatcha." Have students identify how elements such as these would be expressed differently in expository prose.
- Students can practice oral language skills by role-playing callers to a radio station.
- Students can practice written language skills by writing letters to radio stations expressing their opinions about the stations' programming.
- Explore with students the ways in which speakers shade meaning through intonation, pauses, and vocal emphasis.

Social Studies Links

- Use news radio broadcasts to explore current events. Ask students to identify news stories in different categories: local, national, and international. Ask students to discuss why these stories are considered news. Refer students to the discussion of news in Part 1.
- Encourage students to research the role of radio in history—its invention and varied uses before the advent of television.
- Some students may want to explore the role of the Voice of America during World War II and the Cold War.
- Many radio stations facilitate a kind of community identity. Ask students to identify and describe any stations that serve this purpose. Ask questions such as these: What features (hosts, commercials, etc.) make this station special? How does this station help the community or neighborhood?

Cooperative Learning

In addition to the various cooperative learning activities and projects in the worktext, Part 2 offers many other opportunities for cooperative learning. Here are a few suggestions.

- Have students work together to research a topic for an information radio program. Then have students role-play a radio show host, guest speaker, and callers who discuss the topic.
- Have students work together to research and write a profile of a popular talk show host. Students should describe the qualities that contribute to the host's popularity.
- Have student groups prepare a survey of local radio stations—the number of stations (AM and FM), the kind of programs offered, and the kinds of audiences to which the programs appeal.

UNIT 1

INFORMATION TALK RADIO
(PAGES 38-41)

Getting Started

Explain that Unit 1 deals with information talk radio. Direct students' attention to the illustration. Ask students to identify the items shown and to describe how the items are used. Ask students who have visited a radio station to describe their experience. Explain that most cities have at least one radio station, and many have two or more. Explain that most countries around the world also have radio stations. Ask students to name other cities and countries in which they have heard radio broadcasts.

Teaching Suggestions

Have students read Unit 1, Information Talk Radio (pages 38-41). Use the following suggestions to highlight important points and reinforce content.

- Discuss information talk radio shows, emphasizing the informational aspect of the shows. Ask students to identify examples of informational talk radio programs they have heard.
- Guide students in reading the play. You may want to have students role-play parts. Note that Dr. Lynn is on the radio—her show is being broadcast while Michelle and Raul are talking. The dialogue of the play switches back and forth between the broadcast and the conversation between brother and sister.
- Discuss the sidenotes and ask students the following questions:
  - Why might people be interested in listening to an information talk radio show?
  - Why might someone be skeptical of an information talk show?
  - Why might people want to tune in to Dr. Lynn's show?
  - Does Dr. Lynn sound like a good host? Why?
  - Why is it easier for callers to ask uncomfortable questions over the phone?
  - How does the way that Dr. Lynn talks to Maria show that she is an expert?
- Discuss the idea that a title alone (such as Dr.) does not necessarily mean someone is an expert. Encourage students to listen carefully to what the person says and to how the person speaks. Mention that a good indicator of a person's expertise is the person's experience. Provide descriptions of experience and ask students to identify which one they would choose as the better expert. For example, would students choose a carpenter who had just finished an apprenticeship and had built a fence or a carpenter who has owned her own business for three years and just remodeled a house? Would students choose a dentist who had written a textbook for training dentists, had his own practice, and taught at a well-known school of dentistry, or would they choose a dentist who had just graduated from dental school and was starting a new practice? Ask students to describe similar discrepancies in experience.
- Ask students to describe experiences of friends, relatives, or acquaintances who have bought something after hearing about it on radio. What convinced the

person to buy the product? Did the product live up to the buyer's expectations?

- Draw students' attention to Raul's comment about a shady talk show host on page 41. Explain that radio "scams" are not that common but do occur. Discuss how these would make some listeners skeptical of talk shows.
- To extend the introduction, have student volunteers perform the play.

Lesson 1

ARE YOU REALLY LISTENING? (PAGES 42-44)

Objective: Students will use critical listening skills in analyzing and evaluating information talk radio.

Getting Started

Ask students to describe situations in which they interpret or analyze what they hear. One example might be a situation in which someone is trying to sell them something. Another example is in a debate. Introduce the term *critical listening* and explain that it is the skill of carefully analyzing what you hear. Ask questions such as these:

- When has critical listening helped you make the decision not to do something?
- When has critical listening helped you decide in favor of something?

Teaching Suggestions

Have students read "Lesson 1: Are You Really Listening?" (pages 42-44). Use the following suggestions to highlight important points and reinforce content.

- Discuss the list of questions on page 44 and

have students relate them to the scenario involving Dr. Lynn on pages 38-41.
- Direct students to read the scenario involving Jeffrey. You may want to have students role-play this scenario.
- Direct students' attention to the first sidenote on page 43. Students might surmise that Jeffrey's show would be aired in the late afternoon or early evening so that high-school teenagers and young adults could tune in.
- For the second sidenote on page 43, discuss tone. Stress that it is not just what Jeffrey says but how he says it. Draw students' attention to the informal, relaxed language, and Jeffrey's way of personalizing the information by describing his own experiences.
- Direct students' attention to the "Language of Thinking" sidenote on page 43. Ask students to describe a time when they analyzed something. What did they analyze? What did they learn? Ask students to describe something they evaluated. How was their evaluation helpful?
- Discuss Jeffrey's advice. Ask questions such as these: Does it make sense? Does it seem realistic? Ask students to paraphrase the advice.

Answers to Questions on Page 44

Students' answers may vary, depending on their experiences and interpretations. Use the following guidelines and answers to help you evaluate students' responses.

1. Students should recognize that Jeffrey's viewpoint is that stocks are not a mystery; they are easy to understand.
2. Students may speculate that other experts might see stocks as complicated or difficult.

3. Jeffrey's main point about buying stocks is to not be afraid.

4. Jeffrey shows he's an expert by describing his experience with stocks and by giving good advice about investing.

5. Some students may say Jeffrey's idea of avoiding big stocks makes the most sense. Some may want more information on how to tell if a company has grown by 20 percent a year for a few years.

6. Some possible advertisers are banks, stockbrokers, financial advisers, accountants.

Lesson 2

THE SPONSOR STRATEGY (PAGES 45-47)

Objective: Students evaluate the credibility of information talk show hosts as sources of information.

Getting Started

Introduce the following words: *sponsor*, *endorse*, *biased*, and *partial*. List the words on the board and invite student volunteers to define the words. Students should understand that a sponsor is a company that pays to have its products advertised on a radio or television program; to endorse a product is to recommend it or speak favorably about it; a biased opinion is slanted against or in favor of something or someone; partial is a synonym for biased.

Teaching Suggestions

Have students read "Lesson 2: The Sponsor Strategy" (pages 45-47). Use the following suggestions to highlight important points and reinforce content.

- Discuss the issue of experts who are paid to endorse a product. Ask students to identify examples from television commercials. Ask questions such as these: Is the person believable even though he or she is paid—sometimes millions of dollars—to endorse a product? Would the advertisement be as convincing if some unknown person were endorsing the product?

- Ask students to identify facts given by Diane that seem to indicate that she is an expert.

- Draw students' attention to the sidenote on page 46. Point out that students can see Diane's biased view by multiplying 38 cents ($.38) by 10,000 to get $3,800, then dividing $15,000 by $3,800 to get 3.9—the number of years Diane implies the new car will last. Point out that most new cars would be expected to last longer than four years. Also have students use the same method to figure the years of use for the used car, 2.6 years. Again, point out that some four-year-old used cars might indeed last longer than three years.

- Ask students to evaluate Diane's advice on what to look for in a used car. Ask if the advice makes sense, based on what students already know about cars.

- Direct students' attention to the "Language of Thinking" sidenote on page 47. Discuss *hidden agenda*. Define *agenda* as a plan for doing something. Ask students for other examples of a hidden agenda. For example, students might refer to Dr. Lynn's pitch for *Today's Teens* magazine on page 41. Ask students if Jeffrey, in Lesson 2, seemed to have a hidden agenda. Students should conclude that he did not, since he was

not selling stocks or advertising himself as a stockbroker, or advertising any product or service.

- Discuss *credibility* and ask students to cite commercials in which they think the speaker has credibility.

Answers to Questions on Pages 46-47

Students' answers may vary, depending on their experiences and interpretations. Use the following guidelines and answers to help you evaluate students' responses.

1. Students may cite the facts Diane gives for the number of used cars bought and what to look for in a used car.
2. No, Diane does not stick to the facts. She gives some biased information and slips into a sales pitch for Columbia Sales.
3. People interested in cars or in buying a used car might find Diane's show interesting.
4. Columbia Sales would want to sponsor Diane's show because she's an expert on used cars.
5. Diane probably presented the advertisement because she was paid by Columbia Sales and because they are "friends" of hers.
6. Some students may feel that Diane loses credibility because she is paid to read the commercial but does not say so; nor does she announce that she is about to give a commercial. Other students may say she does not lose credibility because she is still an expert and her advice is good even though she gives a commercial.
7. Some students may say it is not fair that Diane uses her status as an expert to try to sell cars, especially without telling the audience what she's doing. Others may say that radio audiences expect this kind of behavior from talk show hosts.
8. Possible ideas include listening carefully and

asking questions such as those in the sidenote on page 47.

- For the "Discussion" on page 47, tell students to give reasons for their ratings. Encourage students to listen carefully to viewpoints that differ from their own.

Lesson 3

STATION SURFING (PAGES 48-49)

Objective: Students will note significant similarities and differences between two information talk radio shows.

Getting Started

Discuss the importance of comparing information about stations. Emphasize that listeners make choices all the time, based on comparing one station, piece of music, or musician to another. Ask students to describe their experiences with "surfing" radio or television channels. Ask questions such as these:

- What do you look or listen for when you surf?
- How can comparing help you make a choice?
- How can listening skills help you compare two stations?

Teaching Suggestions

Have students read "Lesson 3: Station Surfing" (pages 48-49). Use the following suggestions to highlight important points and reinforce content.

- Have students follow directions to complete the chart. Discuss the categories on the chart. Explain that *pre-recorded* advertisements often feature professional

speakers or actors rather than the radio show host. Stress that students should listen to at least two programs.

Answers to Your Conclusion

Students' answers will vary, depending on their experiences and interpretations. Encourage students to use the analysis and evaluation techniques they learned in Lessons 1 and 2 as well as some of the categories in the chart to support their choice. Students may, for example, conclude that a program is better because the host has credibility as an expert and does not present the commercials.

Unit Activity
ALL THE NEWS? (PAGE 50)

- In this cooperative-learning activity, student groups compare radio news and print news. If possible, have copies of newspapers handy. Also have a radio or two handy. You may want to have students do this activity as homework.
- Follow up the activity by having groups compare their conclusions about the way each medium presents the news.

Unit Evaluation
(PAGE 51)

Possible responses to the questions follow.

Checking What You Learned:

1. Students should note that hosts may be experts or may interview experts on a topic.
2. Students should mark the first statement. Students should note that critical listeners use analytical skills involving questions such as: What is this about? What supporting evidence is there? Is the evidence valid? What is the purpose?
3. Students should recognize that an expert

may really believe in a product and sincerely want others to try the product. Students should also recognize that experts are paid to promote products.

4. Students should recognize that the information attracts the listeners and the advertisements pay for the show. Students should also mention that the way the advertisements are presented may have an effect on the credibility of the host's information. Students may cite examples such as Dr. Lynn and Diane Connors.

Checking How You Learned:

Have students share and compare their answers. Encourage students to support their ideas with facts and examples.

UNIT 2

"INFLAMMATION" TALK RADIO (PAGES 52-53)

Getting Started

Explain that Unit 2 deals with "inflammation" talk radio. Direct students' attention to the illustration on page 51. Ask students what radio programs they have heard that reflect the ideas shown in the illustration. Explain that many people lump all talk radio together in one category, just called "talk" radio. Point out that there are really two kinds of talk radio: one is information talk radio, which students have explored in Unit 1; the other is more concerned with opinions and feelings than with information. The second kind is what is being called "inflammation" radio in this book.

Discuss the fact that socially and politically charged radio had its beginnings in Boston and

New York in the late 1980s. Mention that inflammation talk shows have had a powerful influence on American politics and society. As an example, mention that in the late 1980s, a host took his talk show microphone to a crack house in Seattle and was able to get the house shut down. In Boston, for another example, a talk show host got people to protest a tax increase and to relocate the proposed site for a prison. Several of the more raucous talk shows have become popular since the 1992 presidential elections.

Teaching Suggestions

Have students read "Unit 2, Inflammation Radio" (pages 52-53). Use the following suggestions to highlight important points and reinforce content.

- Ask students to describe the difference between information talk radio and inflammation talk radio in their own words. Ask students to name examples of each kind of program.
- Guide students in reading the scenario. Point out that underlined words are emphasized just as they would be by many inflammation talk show hosts. You may want to have volunteers role-play segments of the scenario.
- Discuss the sidenote on page 52. Ask students to describe the assumption Jerry Knight makes about his audience.
- The story about the one-legged criminal is not fictional. A radio show host actually discussed this story in a manner very similar to that presented here. Ask students to compare the way the host treats this kind of story and the way the story might appear in a serious newspaper. Ask students how the host's treatment is like that of a tabloid newspaper.

- Discuss the sidenotes on page 53 concerning bias. Ask students to compare Jerry Knight's bias to that of Diane Connors in Unit 1. Ask questions such as these: How are the two hosts alike? How are they different?

Lesson 1

IS THE HOST PLAYING ON AN EVEN FIELD? (PAGES 54-56)

Objective: Students will analyze or evaluate talk show hosts' attitudes toward callers.

Getting Started

Ask students if they know what the metaphor "playing on an even field" means. If necessary, explain that it means playing fairly, or being fair, balanced, and objective.

Mention that some talk show hosts are powerful by virtue of their popularity. The audience for one top host is estimated at 20 million listeners through 660 radio stations around the country. (Eighty percent of talk show hosts, by the way, are men, and only 3 percent of the audience gets on the air.) The topics addressed on a show include "hot" issues such as taxes, welfare, crime, school lunches, affirmative action, and sports. Ask students what topics are currently among the hot topics of discussion on talk radio.

Discuss the idea that the host is the person who runs the show and his or her attitude toward callers adds to the tone of the show. Ask questions such as these:

- Why would people call an inflammation talk radio show host?
- If you disagreed with a host, would you call in and say so? Why or why not?
- What risks do people face by calling in to

an inflammation show? What possible benefits might there be?

Teaching Suggestions

Have students read "Lesson 1: Is the Host Playing on an Even Playing Field?" (pages 54-56). Use the following suggestions to highlight important points and reinforce content.

- Lead students in a discussion of why people seem to like controversy and conflict, especially in the media. Ask questions such as the following:
  - Do you think people enjoy getting angry about certain issues? Why?
  - Are people seriously interested in the topic, or do they see the controversy as a form of entertainment? What are some examples?
- Ask students if they think inflammation talk show hosts deliberately try to stir up people, and if so, what benefit the hosts get out of doing so.
- Discuss the sidenote on page 54. Ask students how inflammation programs might be different if the hosts were objective. For example, how might the tone of the programs change? Would people find the programs as interesting?
- Draw students' attention to the Language of Thinking sidenote. Ask students how they would decide whether a talk show host was just trying to be persuasive or was using propaganda.
- You may want to have students role-play the scenario with Phyllis, Damond, and Claudia.
- Discuss the sidenote on page 55 concerning loaded words, name calling, and hasty generalizations. Ask students to describe how these techniques might be misleading or even hurtful.

Answers to Questions on Pages 55-56

Students' answers may vary, depending on their experiences and interpretations. Use the following guidelines to help you evaluate students' responses.

1. Students should conclude that Phyllis was not fair to Damond. She cut him off before he could complete his sentence, then she tried to insult him by implying that he was from another planet.
2. She implied that he was from another planet.
3. Some students may think Damond could argue well against Phyllis. He seems to have some information that would challenge her position. On the other hand, some students may say Phyllis is so rude and overpowering that she would not let Damond speak.
4. Students should recognize that she was not objective because she would not allow someone with an opposing view to speak and her own opinion was biased.
5. Students should recognize Phyllis's positive comments, "Good for you...," "Absolutely...," and, "I could use more callers like you!"
6. Some students may say yes, because they'd like to try to get past Phyllis's guard—or they agree with her point. Other students may say no, because they would not want to be trashed by Phyllis.
   - To extend the lesson, have students describe what they might say to Phyllis if they were to call in.

23

Lesson 2

HEARING BOTH SIDES
(PAGES 57-59)

Objective: Students will analyze and evaluate opposing arguments on a topic.

Getting Started

Ask students to identify a controversial issue at school or in their community. Have students describe the two sides of the issue. Explain that being able to make informed decisions involves analyzing and evaluating different opinions about an issue. Review the processes of analyzing and evaluating described in Lesson 1, page 54.

Teaching Suggestions

Have students read "Lesson 2: Hearing Both Sides", pages 57-59. Use the following suggestions to highlight important points and reinforce content.

- Review the concept of a speaker's "main point". Tell students they are probably familiar with the term "main idea" from language arts: it is the most important idea that someone is talking or writing about. Explain that to support a main point, speakers and writers use facts and examples.
- Emphasize being aware of one's bias. Author Scott M. Peck describes a technique called "bracketing". In any new situation, such as meeting new people or receiving new information, Peck advises people to set aside their biases and remain open to the new situation, taking in whatever is to be known or understood. Once the situation is grasped, Peck suggests, people can revert to their biases if they like, but they have at least allowed themselves to see another

point of view. This can be a helpful technique for teens who are often quick to reject unfamiliar ideas and information.

- Ask students to identify Ray Noble's main point.
- Draw students' attention to the sidenote on page 58. Ask students for other examples of misleading statements.
- Have students identify Yolanda's main point.
- Introduce the graphic organizer as a technique for helping students organize information. You may want to have students summarize each person's supporting points under the main points.

Answers to Questions on Page 59

Students' answers may vary, depending on their experiences and interpretations. Use the following guidelines to help you evaluate students' responses.

1. Students should recognize that Ray Noble does not support his main points well because he uses biased and misleading ideas.
2. Students should recognize that Yolanda supports her main points well by using reasonable and logical statements.
3. Students should recognize that hearing both sides of the argument helps them make an informed judgment, like a jury that has heard both sides of a case. Having heard both sides, students can weigh the arguments and decide which they feel is best.
4. Some possible responses include doing research on statistics involving teens and crime, adults and crime, and cities with curfews; students could also survey people in their neighborhoods and in local government.
5. Some students may conclude that an

inflammation talk radio show is not a good place to hear a balanced discussion of a topic because hosts and callers are often biased on one side of an issue.

Lesson 3

FORMING YOUR OWN OPINION (PAGES 60-61)

Objective: Students develop criteria for evaluating talk radio hosts.

Getting Started

Begin a discussion of how students would determine whether a product—such as a used car or a snack food—was good or not good. Refer students to Diane Connors's description of what to look for in a used car. Explain that the information she gave was in the form of *criteria*, or standards by which to judge a used car. Ask students what criteria or standards they would use in judging a snack food or a pair of sneakers.

Teaching Suggestions

Have students read "Lesson 3: Forming Your Own Opinion" (pages 60-61). Use the following suggestions to highlight important points and reinforce content.

- Draw students' attention to the Language of Thinking sidenote and the graphic organizer on page 60. Discuss the meaning of the term *criteria*. Explain that criteria may change, depending on the purpose for which you are judging something.
- Have students discuss the example of establishing criteria for buying a sweater. Ask for examples of criteria for other things, such as a watch, a notebook, a recording, a hero, and a friend.

- Guide students through the chart on page 61. You might have students turn each statement under "criteria" into a question—for example: What is the hosts's tone of voice? Does the host use slang words or name calling? Tell students that if they rephrase the statements as questions, they should still rate a "yes" or "no" answer using the guidelines on page 61, following the chart.
- You may want to have students work cooperatively to fill in the chart on page 61. Provide small radios or ask students to bring in portable radios, if this is at all practicable. Otherwise, students may fill in the chart as a homework assignment.

Unit Activity
DEBATING RADIO

- In this activity, students will debate an issue concerning talk radio. Explain that the first two paragraphs on page 62 are a summary of information from Unit 2. Remind students that talk radio is controversial, and tell them that they will have an opportunity to debate a topic concerning talk radio.
- You may want to have students review the rules of debate at the bottom of page 62 before they carry out their debate. Allow students to choose their own topic for debate from the list or from their discussion.
- Follow up the debate by having students discuss their conclusions.

Unit Evaluation
(PAGE 63)

Checking What You Learned:

1. Students should mark the last choice, "expresses strong opinions about topics".

As an explanation, students may say that the term "inflammation" is a clue to the kind of talk that occurs on this kind of program, which makes it different from other kinds of talk radio.

2. Students should mark the second and third statements, "A biased host does not welcome opposing points of view" and "To persuade an audience, a host may use propaganda methods." As explanation, students may say that the word biased indicates an unfair or one-sided point of view. Students may cite examples from the unit of hosts who used propaganda methods to try to persuade listeners. Some students may say that propaganda is a tool for biased talk-show hosts.

3. Students may cite questions such as these: What is the speaker's main point? How does the speaker support the main point? Are supporting facts, examples, and ideas convincing and sensible? Does the speaker use propaganda techniques? Have I set aside my own biases in order to hear the arguments?

4. Students may say that criteria or standards help them tell whether a host and callers are fair or biased. Criteria can help determine if information is accurate or not.

Checking How You Learned:

Have students share and compare their answers. Encourage students to support their ideas with facts and examples.

ADVERTISING ON RADIO (PAGES 64-65)

Getting Started

Have students describe radio commercials they have heard recently. Ask students how radio commercials differ from one to another and also how they are similar. Ask students to describe the commercials that seem most memorable and to discuss why these commercials are memorable.

Teaching Suggestions

Have students read the feature on advertising on the radio (pages 64-65). You may want to direct students to stop after each section to allow for class discussion. Use the following suggestions to highlight important points and reinforce content.

- You may want to have students role-play the parts in the radio advertisement.
- Have students describe the hidden agenda technique used by Diane Connors in Unit 1, Lesson 2.
- Explain that endorsements or testimonials do not always involve well-known people. Some commercials using this technique are done by unknown actors. In these cases, the idea is that the actor is just an ordinary person, like listeners. Mention that in celebrity endorsements, the celebrity usually says his or her name as part of the commercial.
- As an additional activity, have students keep a radio log for a week. Suggest that students listen to the radio for about 20 or 30 minutes a day. In their log they should record the type of program and the types of products advertised on the program. Then have students analyze the relationship between program content and commercial content.

Encourage students to share their findings.

UNIT 3

MUSIC IN EVERY TIME (PAGES 66-77)

Getting Started

Explain that Unit 3 deals with music—specifically with music broadcast on radio. Direct students' attention to the photo montage on page 66. Discuss the variety of historical events and explain that music played a role in each one. Explain that every culture has its own forms of music. American music includes many categories, including jazz, country, rock, rap, rhythm and blues, orchestral, and folk. Ask students to identify other categories. Students, familiar with other cultures, can describe musical forms from those cultures.

Teaching Suggestions

Have students read "Unit 3, Music in Every Time", pages 66-68. Use the following suggestions to highlight important points and reinforce content.

- Explain that archaeological evidence shows that music was an important part of ancient civilizations such as those of the ancient Egyptians and Greeks. For these civilizations, some dating to 4000 B.C., music was part of religious ceremonies and festivals.
- If possible, play recordings of Native American music to give students a sense of this unique and original American music. Also play recordings of African American spirituals and early American folk songs. Ask students to describe similarities and differences in the music they hear.
- Direct students' attention to the first

sidenote on page 66. Point out that many examples of the music of Native Americans, African Americans, and other ethnic groups has been preserved on audio tape and records. Explain that tape recordings and vinyl disks, as well as memory and community ties, have helped preserve forms of American music.

- Explain that in the 1860s there were white as well as black minstrel troupes. The white troupes usually covered their faces with dark paint and often gave stereotyped performances of African American songs and dances. Black minstrel troupes toured in America and in other countries. Minstrel shows gradually became less popular and were replaced by vaudeville and burlesque.
- Draw students' attention to the sidenote on page 67. Explain that one of the first music superstars in America was an Italian opera singer, Enrico Caruso. His recordings were among the 25 million records Americans bought in 1917. In contrast, point out that by 1995, recordings by Elvis Presley had sold more than half a billion copies.
- Draw students' attention to the sidenote on page 67. Discuss the fact that technological inventions bring frequent changes to media. Just as record producers feared the popularity of radio in the 1920s, radio feared the emergence of long-playing records in the late 1940s and television in the 1950s. Both inventions brought about major changes in radio. Radio developed FM stations to broadcast the high quality recordings available on LPs; and radio became almost entirely a music and talk medium, dropping soap operas, quiz shows, and radio dramas, which were taken over by television.

- To extend work with the unit opener, you may want to have students find additional examples of songs from different eras of American history. Students might assemble lists of songs, examples of song lyrics, and even recordings (borrowed from the public library, for example) for a display of American music.
- Plan a field trip to a local radio station or recording studio. Alternatively, invite a radio program director, disk jockey, or recording engineer to visit the class and discuss broadcast music.

Lesson 1

CATEGORIES OF MUSIC STATIONS (PAGES 69-70)

Objective: Students will develop criteria for evaluating radio stations.

Getting Started

Have a small radio available. Surf stations for a while, asking students to identify the kind of music or talk show being played. Ask students to identify stations they like to listen to.

Teaching Suggestions

Have students read "Lesson 1: Categories of Music Stations" (pages 69-70). Use the following suggestions to highlight important points and reinforce content.

- Have students list formats on the chalkboard and include different categories of music under the appropriate formats. Students should recognize that a format may include more than one category of music.
- Direct students' attention to the sidenote on page 69. Ask students to identify useful

categories from other curriculum areas, such as social studies and science.

- Discuss the term *demographics*. Explain that this is a very important term in advertising because advertising is always aimed at specific audiences. The more advertisers know about their audiences, the better they are able to tailor their advertisements to those audiences. Explain that demographic information may include years of education, occupation, marital status, and number of people in a household. You may want to have students do a brief demographic study of their community or town.

Answers to Questions on Page 70

Students' answers will vary, depending on the specific stations they listen to.

1. Students should indicate whether each station plays Top-40 hits, is a lite station, alternative station, etc.
2. Students should indicate the age group of the target audience for each station.
3. Students should indicate products and services such as clothing stores, soft drinks, car dealers, and repair services.
4. Students should list features such as traffic reports, news reports, contests, give-aways, and extended music segments.
5. Students may include examples of what the DJs say.

For "Your Opinion", students should give supporting reasons for their ratings.

Lesson 2

THE POWER OF MUSIC AS CONTROVERSY (PAGES 71-73)

Objective: Students clarify controversies related to music.

Getting Started

Direct students' attention to the illustration and quotations at the beginning of the lesson. Explain that the quotes represent some of the controversy that has swirled around various forms of music in recent history. Ask students to discuss why music seems to attract such controversy. Ask questions such as these:

- Why do some people find new music so troublesome?
- Do people take music too seriously? Why or why not?
- What kind of power do you think music has?

Share the following description of Elvis Presley by country singer Bob Luman, who was a contemporary of the singer.

"This cat came out in red pants and a green coat and a pink shirt and socks, and he had this sneer on his face and he stood behind the mike for five minutes, I'll bet, before he made a move. Then he hit his guitar a lick, and he broke two strings....So there he was, these two strings dangling, and he hadn't done anything yet, and these high school girls were screaming and fainting and running up to the stage, and then he started to move his hips real slow like he had a thing for his guitar. That was Elvis Presley when he was about nineteen...He made chills run up my back, man, like when your hair starts grabbing at your collar."

Teaching Suggestions

Have students read "Lesson 2: The Power of Music as Controversy" (pages 71-73). Use the following suggestions to highlight important points and reinforce content.

- Draw students' attention to the sidenote on page 71. Point out that groups within societies—and societies themselves—can censor or ban music for different reasons. Explain that sometimes the reasons are bad, as in the case of the Nazi ban on Jewish music, but in other cases the reasons may be valid, as in the case of violent rap music in the United States.
- Discuss each of the components of a song. You may want to have a radio, CD, or tape player handy to play music and have students identify components they hear.
- Ask students to describe some of the critical comments they hear about today's music. Have students discuss whether they think these criticisms are valid or not and why.
- Mention that the music industry has a voluntary system for rating some song lyrics. Some cassettes and CDs contain labels that warn buyers about the content of the lyrics. Some people feel, however, that these efforts by the music industry are not sufficient. In 1995, the American Medical Association demanded mandatory ratings for recordings. The association wants ratings similar to those used in the movie industry. In its call for ratings, the association cited its belief that violent song lyrics prompted children to violent acts.

Answers to Questions on Pages 72-73

Answers will vary, depending on which songs students select.

1. Students should include the complete name of the song and the name of the performer or performers

2. Students should describe each controversial part and what makes it controversial.

3. Comments may include that it is "cool", that it is fun to listen to, that it touches their feelings in some way.

4. Comments may include that it "sends a wrong message", promotes bad behavior or bad relationships between people, or that it is too loud and meaningless.

5. Some students may say the song reflects issues such as homelessness, unemployment, violence, sexism, or racism.

6. Students may cite examples of behavior that may be attributed to the song or efforts to censor or ban the song.

- For the "Discussion" on page 73, tell students to support their opinions with specific reasons. Encourage students to listen carefully to viewpoints that differ from their own.

Lesson 3

IT IS A HIT!
(PAGES 74-75)

Objective: Students will explore implications and consequences of how a recording becomes a hit.

Getting Started

Ask students to identify current hit songs. Have students describe what, in their opinion, helped the song become a hit. Refer students to the list of song features in Lesson

2. Mention that a song becomes a hit by "going gold" or "going platinum". These phrases mean selling a million copies and two million copies, respectively. Refer students to Top-10 lists published in local newspapers and weekly magazines.

Teaching Suggestions

Have students read "Lesson 3: It Is a Hit!" on pages 74-75. Use the following suggestions to highlight important points and reinforce content.

- Discuss the key terms *playlist* and *PD (program director)*. Some students may be under the impression that disk jockeys (DJs) control the selection of songs played on the station. DJ control is increasingly rare as stations compete for audiences, ratings, and advertising dollars. Instead, programming is controlled by program directors and consultants. These are the people responsible for determining the particular mix of music a station plays and for pushing specific songs—scheduling a particular song to be played once an hour, for example.

- Discuss each factor. Ask students to give examples of the involvement of each factor in a hit song.

- Mention that most stations play "singles" from albums. Some single recordings are available on cassettes and CDs, but single selections are meant only to entice people to buy an album. Explain that the term *album* is outdated but still used. The term came into use in the era of 78-RPM records. These records played only about ten minutes on a side. Longer orchestral works took up several records which were packaged together in stiff paper sleeves between two hard covers. This package

became known as an album. During the era of long-playing records, the term continued in use and its meaning was broadened to indicate an extended-play recording that contains several separate songs or tracks.

Answers to Lesson Activity

Students' responses will vary, depending on the songs they select. Students' responses should include a description and evaluation of elements that make up each song, such as lyrics, tempo, and performer.

To extend the activity, have students discuss their opinions and predictions. You may want to suggest that students hold their discussion as if they were a panel of experts on a radio talk show.

As an additional activity, have students research information and write a profile of a recording artist. In their profile, students should describe the qualities that helped the artist become famous.

Unit Activity
PROGRAM DIRECTOR FOR A DAY (PAGE 76)

- In this activity, students will role-play being a radio station program director for a day. Before students begin, you may want to review key terms, *format* and *demographics*. You may also want to have students listen to a radio station for a period of time to gather ideas for programming. Alternatively, you may have students work in groups to brainstorm ideas for programming.
- Follow up the activity by having groups compare their ideas for programming.

Unit Evaluation
(PAGE 77)

Possible responses to the questions follow.

Checking What You Learned:

1. "b" is the most sensible answer. Students may explain that music has stirred controversy many times in this century. Several kinds of music have been banned or discriminated against. Critics of jazz disliked fast tempos, strange melodies, and weird instruments. Critics of rock 'n' roll disliked some of the made-up words and steady beat. Critics of rap disliked some of its antisocial lyrics.

2. Students should mark the first statement, "Categories help you organize information." In explaining this, students may refer to categories of music (such as country, rock, pop), programming formats (such as lite FM, Top-40, and Golden Oldies), and audience demographics (such as age, income, and neighborhood)

3. Students should mention competition among stations; the fact that all stations offer features intended to catch and keep audiences. Some students may also mention competition from television and recordings.

4. In their responses, students should mention the track record of the artist, the tempo of the song, adult themes, call-in requests, and music video.

Checking How You Learned:

Have students share and compare their answers. Encourage students to support their ideas with facts and examples.

PROJECT
GETTING THE MESSAGE FROM
AUDIO MEDIA (PAGES 78-81)

- Lead into the project by discussing some of the ways people are influenced by radio programs and commercials. If necessary, have students review some of the key points from lessons in this part. A summary of the Part 2 content appears on the first page of this project (page 78). In addition to the suggestions listed on page 78, you may want to have students include in their survey the influence of radio commercials on listeners' buying habits.

- The following questions may help you evaluate students' performance on the project: Were students able to work together to generate appropriate questions for the survey? Were students able to organize their questions into a survey form that could be used to gather information? Were students able to conduct the survey effectively, using phonecalls and personal interviews? Were students able to apply tools of analysis and evaluation in interpreting the results of their survey? Were student groups able to share their results with other groups and provide effective feedback?

FOCUS ON TELEVISION AND MOVIES
INTRODUCTION TO PART 3 (PAGES 82-83)

Getting Started

To begin the discussion, ask students to name their favorite movies and television shows. Ask them for reasons they might watch TV or a movie (including movies on a VCR). If they do not mention such reasons as to relax, to keep up with their friends, or to put aside their own problems, suggest these reasons. Ask what students get from watching movies and TV that they do not get from any other activities.

Reading the Text

Have students read the introduction to Part 2, on pages 82-83. You may want to direct students to pause after each section to consider such key questions as these:

- The author mentions the "long-lasting power" of movies and TV shows. What movies or TV shows still mean a lot to you after a long time? What is special about them?
- The author says that in a tough world, film and TV give viewers "as many happy endings as they like." Many people criticize films and TV for being escapist. Others say that a little escapism cannot hurt. How can getting away from real-life problems for a while be a good thing? When can escaping from problems become a problem in itself?

Programming

- What persuasive messages have you noticed in films and television shows you have watched? How did the messages affect the way you felt about the films or shows?
- What informative shows do you recall watching now or in the past? In what ways did they seem to try to be entertaining as well?

Audience

- What other forms of entertainment do you think might be as popular as watching movies or TV? How might you find out this information?
- How do you think differences in age, gender, or way of life might affect which films or TV shows people see? How might TV and film producers use such information to plan their shows and films?

Funding

- Since advertisers pay so much for TV commercial time, how much power might they have over the shows' content? What might advertisers ask a program's producers to show or not to show?
- Another way that movie companies earn money is from merchandising. Manufacturers pay movie companies for the right to use the movie's name or the faces of movie characters on products. For instance, the producers of *Batman* issued over 160 licensing agreements. The movie earned about $50 million from merchandising alone. What other examples of merchandise tied in to a specific film can you recall?

Impact

- The author mentions that many people copy stars' clothing and behavior. What examples of this can you think of?

Critical Issues

- Should there be tougher limits on what TV and movies can show? Why or why not?
- How would you answer the question: Will this limit the free spread of ideas in the future? What reasons can you give for your answer?

SPECIAL STRATEGIES AND ACTIVITIES

Teaching activities for each unit of Part 3 of the worktext are provided in the pages that follow. The specific suggestions below will assist you in teaching ESL/LEP students, in linking the material with language arts and social studies curricula, and in using cooperative learning.

ESL/LEP Strategies

- Continue using the KWL technique to present new material to students. Ask students what they already know about movies or TV shows. This may include American films and TV shows or productions from elsewhere. Ask what students would like to know about how or why TV shows and films are made. After students read the text, have them summarize its main points.
- If possible, pair ESL/LEP students with native speakers or students who have become more fluent readers. Encourage students to ask about information or wording that they do not understand.
- For years people throughout the world have used American films and TV shows as tools for learning English. Encourage students to watch films or TV programs likely to increase their fluency. These might include evening news programs and videotapes of classic films. Ask students to describe or summarize these productions.

Language Arts Links

- TV shows as well as films provide an opportunity to discuss such story elements as plot and characterization. Students can analyze editorial segments on TV news shows to see whether opinions are logically presented and supported by facts. They might examine TV commercials to see what is implied without being stated directly.
- Students might write a TV or movie "ten best" list in which they briefly explain the reason each item has made it to their list of favorites.

Social Studies Links

- Use movies set in other times to examine the role of accuracy in film. Have students research an actual person or event shown in a historical film and compare the film with the actual history. Discuss such questions as these: Is it all right for a film to change historical fact for the sake of good storytelling? What responsibility might viewers have before they form an opinion about the historical person or event? What benefits do viewers get from watching a historical film even if some details are changed or left out?
- Have students investigate current events as they are shown on TV news programs. Discuss questions such as these: How do the three kinds of channels—broadcast, cable, and public—compare in terms of

the amount of detailed coverage they give? How do local news programs differ from national programs in terms of the amount of hard news they deliver?

Cooperative Learning

- Have students work together in small groups to create scripts for TV ads for one product geared to each of these audiences: children from 8 to 12 years old, teenagers, young women, young men. When students have completed their scripts, have them explain how they tailored each ad for its audience.

- Have student groups interview people from several age groups: older adults, young adults, teenagers, and children from 8 to 12 years old. Have them ask each person what they think is good about television and what is bad about it. Group members should discuss their results and see whether there is any grouping of answers: Do most older adults tend to hold similar opinions? Do most children?

- Have students work together to plan a TV newsmagazine show similar to *20/20* or *CBS Sunday Morning*. The show should contain a mixture of hard news and soft news. Students should plan the topics and decide how much time the show will spend covering each topic. Students should also decide on the ideal types of products that would be advertised during commercial breaks. If there is time, students might write part or all of the show's script.

UNIT 1

TELEVISION: LET ME ENTERTAIN YOU (PAGES 84-85)

Getting Started

Explain that Unit 1 deals with television. Point out that most TV channels, whether funded by subscription fees (some cable channels) or advertising (many cable channels and most broadcast channels) depend on popularity with viewers. One way to measure how well shows are doing is ratings. Students may be familiar with ratings, supplied by independent research companies such as the A.C. Nielsen company, which uses various techniques to measure audience size. If possible, display a ratings page from a recent newspaper or *TV Guide*. Ask students why they think TV producers might worry about their shows' ratings. Tell students that they will explore the connnection between ratings, advertisers, and which shows are picked up or dropped by a TV network.

Teaching Suggestions

Have students read pages 84-85 of "Unit 1, Television: Let Me Entertain You". Use the following suggestions to highlight important points and reinforce content.

- List key terms on the chalkboard, including *network, commercial time,* and *prime time*. Have students define these terms in their own words. (Note: Lesson 1 of this unit will define the terms *comedy* and *drama* and explore these two genres in greater depth.)

- Discuss Tiger Hansen's mention of the 18-49 age group by pointing out the sidenote about market research. Have students discuss the question posed in the sidenote.

- Point out the first sidenote on this page. Ask students whether they have ever noticed that several TV shows seemed to have the same idea—for instance, a family with many children being taken care of by the oldest ones. Ask students how they would interpret this, knowing what they know now about how shows are programmed.

- Tell students that in the 1975 TV season, the three main networks introduced twenty-seven new series. Only five of these shows were renewed the following year. In 1994, twenty-eight shows were created, and seven survived the year. In recent years, only about one fourth of the new shows have survived each year. Have students discuss what effect these facts might have on the people who are planning a new season's programs.

Lesson 1

IN SEARCH OF REAL LIFE ON TV (PAGES 86-88)

Objective: Students analyze and evaluate the program content of television comedies and dramas and explore the use of stereotypes in such programs.

Getting Started

Ask students to name regular TV series that have fictional characters and a storyline. List these shows on the chalkboard. Ask questions such as these:
- Which of these shows stress humor?
- Which shows stress action, mystery, or dramatic situations?
- Which shows usually end with problems working out?

- Which shows, if any, end in the middle of a surprising story twist?
- Which shows do you usually watch? What keeps you watching week after week?

Teaching Suggestions

Have students read "Lesson 1: In Search of Real Life on TV" on pages 86-88. Use the following suggestions to highlight important points and reinforce content.

- Ask students to review the shows they listed earlier and categorize them as comedies or dramas. Ask whether any shows seem harder to categorize neatly, and why this is so.

- Tell students that a TV writer and producer, Larry Gelbart, once said, "It's very hard for us to compete in our everyday lives with television. We're not as well made up, we're not as in focus, we're not as glamorous."
  Ask students to explain what this statement means. Ask them how the statement applies to TV stereotypes such as the ones in the word game.

- Tell students that the TV episodes they choose to watch should be on a channel that shows commercials. The channel could be either broadcast or cable.

- Before students watch the TV episodes, stress that they will be watching critically. This means that before they start, they will plan what to watch for. Writing down their plan will help them stick to it.

- Direct students to fill out the form on page 88 independently. You may want to have students compare and discuss their findings in pairs, in small groups, or with the entire class.

- Have students use the their data to compute the actual length of an hour

show and a half-hour show, minus commercial time. Have them discuss their reactions to their findings.

- Before students begin the "Discussion", review with them procedures for a large group discussion. These include giving others a chance to speak without interruption, raising their hands if they want to speak, and listening carefully to other viewpoints. At the end of the discussion, work with students to summarize the most important points they thought were made during the discussion.

Lesson 2

A VOTE FOR ME IS A VOTE FOR AMERICA (PAGES 89-90)

Objective: Students explore the role of television in politics and compare two politicians' statements on opposite sides of an issue.

Getting Started

Ask students whether they remember seeing any politicians on TV. Ask questions such as the following: Were these politicians running for office, or did they already hold office? On what kinds of shows—for example, news shows or talk shows—did they appear? Were any of these appearances in campaign ads? What details do you remember from these TV appearances?

Teaching Suggestions

Have students read "Lesson 2: A Vote for Me Is a Vote for America" on pages 89-90. Use the following suggestions to highlight important points and reinforce content.

- Ask whether students have ever heard of a press secretary. Explain that many high-

ranking political officials, such as the President, governors, and mayors, have a press secretary to coordinate the official's contacts with reporters and with the public. Ask students why a politician would employ a person whose only job is to present the official to the media.

- Discuss the "Language of Thinking" sidenote on page 90. Then have students read the two political statements. Ask them to notice whether either of the statements contain facts to support the politicians' opinions. Have students be on the alert for data such as money amounts that show statements to be factual.

Answers to Questions on Page 90

1. The only fact given is that tax cuts will cut many government programs that fund crimefighting, schools, and road repairs. Even that fact is not accompanied by supporting data.

2. Students should recognize that nothing in either statement is enough to base a decision on, because no specific information is given. Both statements appeal to viewers' feelings.

3. Students should realize that TV often gives insufficient information about political issues. Also, this information may be strongly slanted to support one viewpoint.

4. Answers may vary. Students should cite one or more of the following: specific data about whom tax cuts will benefit most, information about how government programs will be affected by a tax cut, and a more complete, balanced argument about the possible benefits and dangers of a tax cut.

Lesson 3

AND NOW A LATE-BREAKING STORY (PAGES 91-92)

Objective: Students draw conclusions about the usefulness of various kinds of television news shows as a source of information on current events.

Getting Started

Ask students to recall times they have watched a major news event covered on TV. Ask for examples of such events. Remind students that often in those situations a reporter has broadcast directly from the scene of the event. Although newspaper and magazine reporters may also have access to instant news bulletins, what advantage might TV have in terms of relaying bulletins to the public?

Teaching Suggestions

Have students read "Lesson 3: And Now a Late-Breaking Story" on pages 91-92. Use the following suggestions to highlight important points and reinforce content.

- Point out that most news shows, including evening news reports, begin and end with theme music. A few years ago, some theme music for NBC news programs was composed by John Williams. Williams is the composer of music for such movies as *Star Wars*, *Superman*, and *Jaws*. Ask what this fact seems to show about what the lesson calls "the line between news and entertainment".
- Help students identify news shows of each type to watch for their evaluation. Students should not confuse news analysis or interview shows such as *Meet the Press* with other Sunday morning shows such as

CBS Sunday Morning, which is a lighter newsmagazine show. Another news analysis show, *Nightline*, is on late at night but might be taped for daytime viewing.

- Encourage students to fill out their evaluations individually and then work with a partner or small group to compare findings.
- Point out that many of the news analysis programs feature interviews with high-ranking public officials, such as U.S. senators and representatives, governors, and cabinet members. Ask why such people might agree to appear on these programs.

Lesson 4

TV NATION (PAGES 93-94)

Objective: Students make generalizations about the influence of television in their own lives and on American culture.

Getting Started

Ask students whether they have ever heard of the terms *boob tube* or *couch potato*. Have students define these terms in their own words. Ask why they think such critical terms exist for people who watch TV heavily. Ask whether students know anyone who does not have a television set. What do those people do for entertainment instead of watching TV?

Teaching Suggestions

Have students read "Lesson 4: TV Nation" on pages 93-94. Use the following suggestions to highlight important points and reinforce content.

- Have students discuss the quotations that begin the lesson. Ask whether they think the first statement is meant in a positive way or a negative way. Ask whether they agree or disagree with the second statement, and why.

- After students have worked together to fill out the chart about fads, have groups share and compare their charts.

- Ask students whether they remember times during their childhood when they pestered their parents to buy them something they wanted because they saw it on TV. Have students recall what they learned earlier in this unit about the role of commercials in TV. Invite them to make a connection between their own behavior and this role. Would they call such behavior an effect of television? Why or why not?

- Point out the "Mediawise" sidenote on page 93. Ask students whether they would count product placements as advertising for a product. Ask students how they would use the information from this sidenote the next time they watch TV.

- As students prepare for their debate, encourage them to make notes on what they plan to say. Remind them to give specific examples, when possible, to back up their arguments. They should also try to anticipate points that the opposition might make, so that they can address these points in their own argument.

- After students work individually to answer the questions, have volunteers summarize their answers for the class.

Unit Activity
TAKING A LOOK AT THE TV YOU WATCH (PAGE 95)

- In this cooperative-learning activity, student groups examine their TV viewing habits. They will recall shows they have watched for several lessons in this unit as well as local TV listings from a newspaper or magazine.

- Follow up on the activity by having groups compare their findings and answers to the questions. Ask students how they might change their TV viewing habits in the future.

Unit Evaluation
(PAGE 96)

Possible responses to the questions follow.

Checking What You Learned:

1. Students should disagree. Even hard news programs such as the evening news feature some soft news segments.

2. The first statement is true. With regard to the second statement, students have already encountered two biased politicians' speeches and have discussed how politicians use TV to get their viewpoints across.

3. Commercial time on high-rated shows may cost more, but commercials on these shows are seen by more viewers. This means that more people are likely to see and maybe buy the product being advertised.

4. One way TV influences the way people think is to make them informed about events around the world. TV also exposes people to different environments and different ways of life. TV affects people's actions by influencing them to follow fads, including fashion and slang. TV also affects people's actions by influencing them to buy products that are advertised in commercials.

Checking How You Learned:

Have students share and compare their answers. Encourage students to support their ideas with facts and examples.

ADVERTISING IN TELEVISION (PAGES 97-98)

Getting Started

Have students make a list of jingles or dialogue from TV commercials that they know by heart. Ask them why they think these things stick in their minds. Ask how they think these elements cause people to remember the brands of products being advertised.

Teaching Suggestions

Have students read the feature on advertising on television (pages 97-98). You may want to direct students to stop after each section to allow for class discussion. Use the following suggestions to highlight important points and reinforce content.

- Tell students that, like some TV shows, some commercials try to be artistic and unusual. Ask students for examples of commercials that stand out because they are especially entertaining. Ask what effect this kind of advertising might have on whether TV viewers might think highly of the product in the commercial.
- Point out that one kind of commercial that they learned about when they studied radio is even more effective on TV. This is the celebrity endorsement. Such endorsements usually feature an actor, a model, a recording artist, or an athlete. Celebrities can make hundreds of thousands or even millions of dollars a year from commercials. Ask students for specific examples of celebrities in TV

commercials. Ask what audiences each celebrity's commercial might be targeting. Why might it be so effective to link a famous name and face to a particular product? What products have students been tempted to buy because of a celebrity endorsement? Why?

- As an additional activity, have students speculate on celebrities they can think of who are not currently featured in TV commercials and have them decide what products they might most effectively promote. Have students tell what audiences a commercial with each celebrity would most likely target. Students might prepare a script for a celebrity commercial.

UNIT 2

MUSIC ON TELEVISION (PAGES 99-121)

Getting Started

Explain that Unit 2 deals with a specific form of television, music television. This includes cable channels such as MTV and VH1 that play chiefly music videos. Ask students whether they have watched music videos on those channels. Ask how music videos compare to other TV programs. What traits of music videos make them interesting to watch and hard to forget? What age group do students think would be the most frequent viewers of music channels? Tell students that they will explore what music channels show, including videos and nonmusic programs, and will examine ways in which these channels design their programming and commercials to appeal to specific audiences.

Teaching Suggestions

Have students read pages 99-100 of "Unit 1, Music on Television". Use the following suggestions to highlight important points and reinforce content.

Introductory Paragraph

- Be sure students are aware of how cable TV differs from broadcast TV. Explain that cable TV signals are relayed by cables, not over open airwaves. Therefore a home must have a special receiver to get cable signals. Cable viewers pay a monthly subscription fee to receive cable service. This money finances some of the costs of making cable programs. Many cable channels, including music channels, also run commercials to fund their expenses. Because cable channels have subscribers instead of random viewers, they can appeal to specialized audiences. Have students help you list some of the specialized channels available (for example, Nickelodeon for children, ESPN for sports fans, The Weather Channel, the Sci-Fi Channel, and of course, MTV).

Beginnings

- Ask students whether seeing a music video has ever gotten them to buy a single or an album by a particular artist or group. Ask whether they would be more likely to be attracted to a song by radio play or by a video of it. Ask why they answered as they did.

Not Just Music

- (Note: The audience breakdown for music television will be examined in greater depth in Lesson 2.) Remind students of what they learned about market research in Unit 1.

Help students recall that this kind of research can help advertisers as well as TV producers target their messages to viewers. Ask students what kinds of advertisers might air commercials during programs designed for a largely teen audience.

Feature

- After students read about the steps of the video-making process, ask which elements of that process most surprised them. Then call their attention to the "MediaWise" sidenote. Ask whether they can think of any commercials or movies that seem to have been based on the music video style.
- Students may be aware of what special effects are (actions or events that probably couldn't happen in real life but can be shown on film). Have students supply examples of special effects they have seen in music videos.
- Ask whether students have ever been impressed with a song because of the video's unusual special effects or style, only to discover that the song played by itself was ordinary.

Lesson 1

WHAT IS ON MUSIC TELEVISION (PAGES 101-102)

Objective: Students examine the programming mix of music video channels, including nonmusic shows, and evaluate these programs in terms of their popularity.

Getting Started

Ask students whether they have ever been satisfied watching just one kind of program on television—even if that one kind of program is

fast-moving music videos. Ask questions such as these:

- Why might a channel supported by advertisers want to program many types of shows?
- If you ran a channel that targeted teenagers and young adults, what else, besides music videos, might you program?

Teaching Suggestions

Have students read "Lesson 1: What Is on Music Television?" on pages 101-102. Use the following suggestions to highlight important points and reinforce content.

- Ask how a cartoon show on a music channel might be different in content or visual style from a cartoon show designed for young children.
- Have students who are familiar with music channels describe some of the specific shows that air on such channels. Ask what elements of those shows seem designed especially to appeal to teenagers or young adults.
- Before students conduct the class poll, tell them that the favorite shows they choose need not be on a music channel. They can name shows from broadcast channels or other cable channels also.
- As students discuss why certain shows and videos are popular among class members, ask which of these shows might be enjoyed by people of other age groups. What traits make these shows appealing to a broader audience? Also ask what different shows people from another age group—for example, children from 7 to 9 years old—might choose as their favorites.
- Before students begin the "Discussion", review the procedures for a large group discussion. These include giving others a

chance to speak without interruption, raising their hands if they want to speak, and listening carefully to other viewpoints. At the end of the discussion, work with students to summarize the most important points they thought were made during the discussion.

Lesson 2

WHO WATCHES MUSIC TELEVISION (PAGES 103-104)

Objective: Students assess how effectively music channels target programming and commercials to their audience of teenagers and young adults.

Getting Started

Have students think about commercials they feel have been targeted to them as teenagers. Ask questions such as these:

- What products do these commercials sell?
- Do any of these commercials star a celebrity who you or other people your age admire? Give several examples.
- What visual effects—bright colors, animation, unusual special effects, quick cuts—do these commercials use? Give specific examples.
- What kinds of music do these commercials use?

Teaching Suggestions

Have students read "Lesson 2: Who Watches Music Television?" on pages 103-104. Use the following suggestions to highlight important points and reinforce content.

- Point out that in recent years, programmers and advertisers on broadcast TV networks have featured a more varied

42

mix of people, including some older people, people from different ethnic groups, and people with disabilities. However, while most broadcast TV networks want to appeal to a mass audience, music channels have a far narrower audience segment in mind. How might that difference be seen in the kinds of people shown on music television? What real-world elements are likely to be missing on a channel targeting mainly people from 13 to 34?

- Remind students of the discussions they had in Unit 1 about stereotypes. Have students think about the overall view of girls and women on music videos. Would they call this view stereotyped? If so, in what way? Is stereotyping of women and girls more common in certain types of music videos?

- Direct students to the "MediaWise" sidenote about MCI's link with an MTV program. Ask students how this information will affect the way they view music television programs and promotions in the future.

- If not everyone in your class has access to music channels, expand students' assessment of commercials to include commercials on other channels.

Answers to Questions on Page 104

Note: Answers to questions 1-3 are based on opinion and will vary greatly.

4. Possible characteristics students might cite: interested in new things, not easy to impress, comfortable with computers, eager to look good and be popular. Advertisers would probably want to know what makes us feel less insecure about our looks or popularity, what activities we like, how much money we can spend, and how easily

we react to peer pressure.

- Before students begin the "Discussion", review with them procedures for a large group discussion. These include giving others a chance to speak without interruption, raising their hands if they want to speak, and listening carefully to other viewpoints. At the end of the discussion, work with students to summarize the most important points they think were made during the discussion.

Lesson 3

THE POWER OF MUSIC TELEVISION (PAGES 105-106)

Objective: Students explore the impact of music television and evaluate whether this impact is good or bad.

Getting Started

Ask students to consider what they or their friends do or believe because of the influence of music videos and other music channel shows. Ask questions such as these:

- What recordings have you bought because you saw the music video on TV?
- How many of your favorite performers did you first hear on a music channel?
- What products have you bought because you saw them advertised on a music channel?
- What dances have you and your friends learned about from a music video or other music channel program?
- What clothing styles have you adopted after seeing them on a music channel?
- What slang or behavior have you or your friends imitated after seeing it on a music channel?

43

- What have you learned about politics or other issues from a music channel?

Teaching Suggestions

Have students read "Lesson 3: The Power of Music Television" on pages 105-106. Use the following suggestions to highlight important points and reinforce content.

- Ask students who watch music channels whether watching these channels gives them a sense of belonging with other teenagers across the country. Ask what other activities give them such a sense of belonging.
- Have students consider the term *vidiot* as used on page 105. Have them discuss the claim that music television turns many teenagers into vidiots.
- Direct students' attention to the "MediaWise" sidenote about the MTV committee that rejects some videos for airing. Have students answer the question asked in the sidenote.
- After students have written their responses to the questions they have chosen and described something that has been influenced by music television, have them work in groups to compare their statements.

Unit Activity
PLAN A MUSIC VIDEO
(PAGE 107)

- In this cooperative learning activity, students work alone or with a small group to plan a music video's storyboard.
- Follow up on the activity by having groups share their video plans. If a video camera is available, groups might record and show their video.

Unit Evaluation
(PAGE 108)

Possible responses to the questions follow.

Checking What You Learned:
1. Students should choose phrase "b".
2. The first and third statements are true. The second statement is false because music videos are like short movies and require the efforts of dozens of people.
3. Advertisers are attracted to music television because it has so many viewers. Also, most of these viewers are young and hip, between the ages of 13 and 34.
4. Student answers may vary greatly. Some students may agree with the statement. Others may disagree, pointing out that music channels sometimes play older videos of songs that are no longer on the charts. Students who disagree with the statement may also cite innovative videos such as early Michael Jackson videos that are still watched and admired for their artistic value.

Checking How You Learned:

Have students share and compare their answers. Encourage students to support their ideas with facts and examples.

UNIT 3

MOVIES: THE WORLD OF ILLUSION (PAGES 109-111)

Getting Started

Explain that Unit 3 covers movies. Have students consider what traits make movies appealing to them. On the chalkboard, begin a list of students' favorite movies. Ask students to differentiate between movies that

are their favorites right now and longtime favorites that they still enjoy watching, perhaps on video. Ask what traits make these movies such longtime favorites. Tell students that in this unit they will investigate how movies are made and how they are promoted in order to attract audiences.

Teaching Suggestions

Have students read pages 109-111 of "Unit 1, Creating the Illusion". Use the following suggestions to highlight important points and reinforce content.

Creating the Illusion

- Mention that although many films begin with a script (also called a screenplay) that is original, others are based on a story from a book, comic book, or TV show. Ask what advantage a movie, based on an already existing story, might have for audience appeal.
- Ask students how many behind-the-scenes jobs in filmmaking they are aware of. Students who enjoy science fiction or horror films may know about special effects experts or makeup artists.
- Students may not see the advantage of being a financial backer for a film. Explain that studios and other backers usually give money to make a film in return for a promise of a percentage of the money the movie makes. If a movie is a hit, backers might earn back much more than the amount of their original investment. Of course, many movies are not hits. Ask how this high-risk element might affect the kinds of movie ideas backers might agree to support.

Pre-Production

- Tell students that most American movies used to be filmed in film studios, usually in Hollywood. Today, many movies are filmed partly or entirely *on location*, or in real settings. American films have been shot on location all over the world. Sometimes *sets*—settings such as a space ship or a castle—are built either on location or in a studio. Have students name movies that seem to have elaborately built sets. Recent examples include *Star Trek*: *Generations* and *Batman Forever*.

Production

- Point out that many segments that take only a few moments of a movie might take hours or even days to film. This is because a director often needs to ask for many retakes of the same shot if the first take doesn't look right.

Post-Production

- After students read about the post-production process, point out that although the editor has a great deal of influence on a movie's final shape, other people have greater power to decide what the movie's *final cut* looks like. Usually the movie's producers have the most say over the final cut. A few directors, such as Spike Lee and Steven Spielberg, have this power. Why might people try so hard to get this power?

Lesson 1

HOW DO MOVIE MAKERS GET YOU TO GO TO A MOVIE? (PAGES 112-114)

Objective: Students analyze the techniques movie makers use to attract audiences.

Getting Started

Ask students what features might attract them to theaters to see new movies. Ask questions such as the following:

- Are there certain stars whose movies you usually go to see? Who are they?
- If a movie is a sequel to another movie you enjoyed, do you look forward to seeing it? Why?
- What influence do your friends have on whether you go to see a new movie?
- What influence do magazine reviews, ads, or features about a movie, have on your movie plans?
- What effect does watching a short preview of a movie have on your movie plans?

Teaching Suggestions

Have students read "Lesson 1: How Do Movie Makers Get You to Go to a Movie?" on pages 112-114. Use the following suggestions to highlight important points and reinforce content.

- Remind students of what they have learned about market research in the units on television and music television. Ask whether market research might be useful for movie makers too. Ask what movie makers might want to learn about people and their tastes.
- After students examine the list of promotion strategies that movie makers

use, ask whether they have ever been disappointed in a movie they went to see because of its advance promotion. Invite them to cite specific elements that made them dislike the movie.

Answers to Questions on Pages 113-114

Students' answers may vary greatly. As you discuss the answers with the class, you might stress the point that people's interest in current and upcoming movies does not happen by coincidence. People are made aware of these movies by carefully planned and expensive advertising campaigns. This does not mean that the movies are bad, or that the advertising is false. In fact, many movies are entertaining, and some can be works of art. However, students should be aware that a movie is a product that is being sold by its producers. It is up to viewers to decide how to respond to promotional campaigns.

- Before students begin the "Discussion", review the procedures for a large group discussion. These include giving others a chance to speak without interruption, raising their hands if they want to speak, and listening carefully to other viewpoints. At the end of the discussion, work with students to summarize the most important points they thought were made during the discussion.

Lesson 2

EVALUATING MOVIES (PAGES 115-117)

Objective: Students compare two differing views of the same movie and develop criteria by which they can evaluate movies.

Getting Started

Ask students whether they have ever read movie reviews in a newspaper or magazine or seen a movie review on TV. Ask questions such as the following:

- What are some movies that you have gone to see because of a good movie review? Were you satisfied or disappointed?
- What movies have you stayed away from because you read or heard a bad review?
- What would you want to know about a movie to help you decide whether or not to see it?

Teaching Suggestions

Have students read "Lesson 2: Evaluating Movies" on pages 115-117. Use the following suggestions to highlight important points and reinforce content.

- Explain that there are many sources of movie reviews or evaluations. Current movies are usually reviewed in newspapers, magazines, and on radio or TV. Another source of movie information is books designed for the home video market. These books describe and evaluate movies available on video. Why might such books be useful?
- Before students begin writing their movie description, ask them to think about what features of a movie they usually are most aware of as they watch and what features they best remember afterward. In what movies have they noticed and thought about the theme? What makes cinematography stand out for them? In what movies have they been aware that the plot didn't make sense? In what movies have they been aware that the plot caught them up and ended in a satisfying way?

- As students plan their reviews, point out that the purpose of a review (or at least a favorable one) is to get viewers interested in a movie. Therefore, although a review might give some plot details, it should not just retell the whole story. Also, ask why a reviewer might not reveal surprise twists or endings.
- After students write their reviews, encourage them to share their reviews with a partner or group. If more than one person reviewed a movie, have students compare the reviews.

Lesson 3

THE INFLUENCE OF MOVIES (PAGES 118-119)

Objective: Students examine the influence of movies on society, particularly with regard to violence.

Getting Started

Ask students to give examples of film fashions, hairstyles, or dialogue that have influenced them or their friends. Ask questions such as the following:

- How does the fact that movies can set trends prove that movies have an influence on people who see them?
- What other elements from movies might influence the way viewers act or think?

Teaching Suggestions

Have students read "Lesson 3: The Influence of Movies" on pages 118-119. Use the following suggestions to highlight important points and reinforce content.

- Point out that salaries for the stars of blockbuster action films can be as high as

$15-20 million *per movie*. The movies themselves can earn $200 million in ticket sales just in the United States and hundreds of millions more internationally, from video sales, and from product merchandising. Ask how the level of money involved might affect the argument about changing the content of such films.

- Point out that to many people, the key issue in the violence debate is whether a cause-and-effect relationship exists between violence in films and violent behavior in society. To prepare students for their role-play, ask them to think about what points they might make on both sides of this issue.

- Explain that even people who dislike violent films are sometimes against limiting them because this would be a form of censorship. Ask how movie makers' freedom of expression (and viewers' freedom to see what they want) could be protected while the issue of violence in movies is addressed. (For instance, students might consider the "MediaWise" sidenote on ratings.)

- Students might work in small groups on their role-plays. You might want to have one or more groups present their role-plays for the entire class. Afterward, ask students what they learned by "becoming" the different characters. Ask students what they learned from viewing the role-plays.

Answers to Questions on Page 119

Students' answers may vary, depending on their point of view on the issue. As you discuss the answers in class, you may want to stress the following points:

- It may be interesting to observe whether students' gender seems to affect the way

they answer question 1.

- Students may say that violent films are popular because they are exciting and fast-moving. Also, people who feel powerless in real life can identify with the hero who demolishes bad guys. You might present the term *catharsis*—a release of emotional tensions that brings a relief. Many people find that exciting movies of all kinds help them get the tensions of daily life out of their systems. However, are some films so violent that they cannot be justified even by these benefits?

- Help students explore the cause-effect aspect of violence in movies, especially on children. Point out that many scientific studies seem to show that exposure to violent actions desensitizes viewers so that witnessing violent acts upsets them less. Yet many people watch violent movies and do not repeat the behavior in real life.

- Ask for suggestions for cutting down on violence in movies without making movies dull. Supply or elicit examples of exciting movies that are not overly violent. (Examples include the *Star Trek* and *Star Wars* movies.)

Unit Activity
AN IDEA FOR A MOVIE (PAGE 120)

- In this cooperative learning activity, students work individually to plan a movie and write a scene from the movie.

- Follow up on the activity by having volunteers share their movie plans with the class. If possible, allow some students to cast and rehearse their scenes and then act them out.

Unit Evaluation
(PAGE 121)

Possible responses to the questions follow.

Checking What You Learned:

1. Students should disagree. They have read that producers use a variety of promotional methods including trailers in theaters and on television, ads in newspapers and magazines and on the radio, posters and trailers in video stores, and sneak previews.

2. The second statement is true. A movie's sound-track is prepared during the post-production stage, not during the development stage. An ideal movie subject would appeal to a broad audience including both younger and older viewers.

3. Movie makers spend a lot to advertise a movie because they want to attract as many viewers as possible.

4. Student answers may vary greatly. Some students may say that a trailer is a better choice because it gives viewers an idea of the style and acting in the movie. Others may say that a review is a better choice because the trailer is made by the movie makers, who are biased in favor of the movie and pick only the best parts to show. The review is written by someone who is not working for the movie company.

Checking How You Learned:

Have students share and compare their answers. Encourage students to support their ideas with facts and examples.

PROJECT
PROGRAMMING TV SHOWS
(PAGES 122-125)

- Begin the project by having students list categories of shows with which they are familiar: comedies, dramas, talk shows, game shows, and so on. Students will be able to refer to this list as they plan their shows. Stress that students will be inventing their own shows, not using shows that already exist. (Of course, their shows can be very close in concept and content to existing shows.) For the schedule, students should provide a brief description of each show, as demonstrated in the example on page 123.

- The following questions may help you evaluate students performance on the project: Were students able to work together to plan a variety of shows and commercials? Were their shows planned to appeal to the audience they thought would tune in at that time of day? Were they able to give good reasons for the commercials they slotted into each program? Did students learn from comparing other groups' schedules with their own?

FOCUS ON COMPUTER BASED MEDIA

INTRODUCTION TO PART 4 (PAGES 126-127)

Getting Started

Begin a discussion by asking students to identify as many uses for computers as they can. Help students recognize that computers are involved in many aspects of daily life, including supermarket check-out counters, traffic signals, telephone systems, banks and other businesses, hospitals, schools, and libraries. Ask students to describe experiences they have had with computers. Explain that computer-based media are media in which computers are the main component. These include CD-ROMs and on-line services.

Reading the Text

Have students read the introduction to Part 4, pages 126-127. You may want to direct students to pause after each section to discuss such key questions as these:

Software and Hardware

- How are today's computers different from the first computers?
- What is *software*? What is *hardware*? What is *multimedia*?

Audience

- Why are young people an important audience for computer-based media?
- What is a computer network?
- What is the Internet?
- Why is a modem necessary in order to use the Internet?

Market

- In terms of funding, how are personal

computers different from broadcast media?
- How do makers of computer hardware and software try to influence buyers?
- Why are computer hardware and software makers eager to influence buyers?

Impact

- The author writes that "Most businesses in the United States depend upon computers to carry out everyday tasks." From your own experience, what are some of these tasks.
- What are some drawbacks of computers.

Critical Issues

- Why is access to computers a big issue?

SPECIAL STRATEGIES AND ACTIVITIES

Teaching suggestions for each section of Part 4 of the worktext are provided in the pages that follow. The specific suggestions below will assist you in teaching ESL/LEP students, in linking the material with language arts and social studies curricula, and in using cooperative learning.

ESL/LEP Strategies

Part 4 contains information that may be especially challenging to ESL/LEP students because it contains technical terms and concepts. The following strategies may be useful:

- Direct students to preview unit features and lessons. Have students read the first sentence of each paragraph, notice any

boldfaced words in the text, and analyze the illustrations. Explain that this procedure helps them become familiar with the content of the feature before they read.

- Suggest that students record any questions they have after previewing the selection. You may want to discuss these questions before students begin reading.
- Pair ESL/LEP students with English-fluent students who can read information aloud in the unit features (including sidenotes).

Language Arts Links

Computer applications offer several opportunities for integrating media-related content into the language arts curriculum. Here are some suggestions:

- Students will learn to follow directions and write directions. In using computer hardware and software, students will be confronted with instructions, both in printed (paper) documentation and on-screen directions. Encourage students to paraphrase directions and make notes about procedures.
- On-line interactivity requires writing skills. Encourage students to practice exchanging ideas on a topic. If on-line services are not available, have small groups of students write, exchange, and respond to notes on a specific topic, using paper. These notes can be posted on a bulletin board so that students can read and respond on a daily basis.
- Suggest that students keep a personal log of tips, information, procedures, and questions as they work with computer-based media. This log can be a resource for longer writing assignments related to

using computer-based media. For example, students can write essays about their experience with on-line services or Internet.

- Encourage students to write reviews or critiques of software and on-line services they use. These reviews can be combined in a class newsletter or magazine devoted to computer-based media.

Social Studies Links

Some CD-ROM products and on-line services provide a wealth of information that can be linked to social studies curricula. Here are some possible links:

- Students can investigate social, cultural, political, and geographic topics using educational CD-ROMS and on-line research. If computers are not available in the classroom or school library, students can use computers at public libraries.
- Suggest that students investigate the effect of computers on industry and other institutions. Mention phrases such as "the computer revolution" and "the electronic revolution". These suggest major changes in industry equivalent to the industrial revolution. How are these revolutions alike? How are they different? Some students may prepare a timeline indicating major computer inventions such as ENIAC, personal calculators, personal computers, portable computers, CD-ROMs, laptop computers, and so on.
- Some students may investigate the role of computers in political polls. Questions to address include these: Why have polls become more prevalent in politics and government? How do computers help make polls more prevalent? Do computers make polls more reliable?

Cooperative Learning

In addition to the various cooperative learning activities and projects in the worktext, Part 4 offers many other opportunities for cooperative learning. Here are a few suggestions.

- Have student groups create and carry out a survey of available computers in their community. The goal is for students to identify computers to which they might have access if a sufficient number of computers are not available in the classroom.
- Have students work in groups to learn about a piece of computer hardware or software. A student group might visit a computer store and interview a sales representative; or students might send away for catalogues and analyze descriptions of various products.
- Have students work in groups to explore a topic through the World Wide Web. Pursuing a topic through the Web involves decision making and intuition as well as information about Web searchers. Students will benefit from a cooperative approach in using the Web.

UNIT 1

PLAYING AND LEARNING WITH MULTIMEDIA (PAGES 128-138)

Getting Started

Explain that Unit 1 deals with multimedia—specifically CD-ROM software. Explain that a wide variety of CD-ROM software exists and that one of the ways to become familiar with some of it is to read reviews of the programs. Tell students that pages 128-129 are set up to resemble a computer magazine in which they would find reviews of CD-ROM programs. You may want to ask students what computer magazines they are familiar with.

Teaching Suggestions

Have students read "Unit 1, Playing and Learning With Multi-Media", pages 128-129. Use the following suggestions to highlight important points and reinforce content.

Build a City From Your CD-ROM

- Some students may already be familiar with the term CD-ROM. Write the term on the board and ask volunteers to define it. Direct students' attention to the sidenote on page 128 for further information about CD-ROMs.
- Ask students to describe their experiences with arcade-type games. Ask their opinion of nonfighting games such as the one described in this article.

More Zap and Zip!

- Ask students to compare CD-ROM game collections to CD audio albums.
- Direct students' attention to the sidenote on page 128. Discuss the popularity of arcade games.

An Exciting Trek Through an Encyclopedia

- Write the key term *interactive* on the board. Ask students to define the word and to describe interactive programs they have used.
- Draw students' attention to the sidenote on page 129 for further information about the term *interactive*. Also discuss the term *hypertext*. Some students may

have encountered this feature in some CD-ROM programs or on the Internet. Ask volunteers to describe their experiences.

An Educational CD-ROM

- Ask students who speak a second language how they learned that language. Ask students how a computer program might help them learn another language.

Lesson 1

HOOKED ON GAMES? EVALUATE! (PAGES 130–132)

Objective: Students will develop criteria for evaluating computer games.

Getting Started

Computer games are extremely popular. The goal of this lesson is to help students evaluate the time they spend with video games and to evaluate the kinds of games they play. By way of background, you may want to share the following information with students.

- In the United States, about 30 million people play computer games. Half of these people are 18 years old or younger.
- In 1995, Sony and Sega introduced new 32-bit video game players. The companies planned to spend more than $100 million in advertising on the two players. Games designed for one player cannot be played on the other player.
- New technology enables the manufacturers to make the video games more sophisticated—more challenging and with more vivid graphics.

Ask questions such as these:

- How much time do you spend playing video games a week?
- Why do you think it might be important to evaluate the time you spend playing games?
- Why do you think it might be important to evaluate the kinds of games you play?

Teaching Suggestions

Have students read "Lesson 1: Hooked On the Games? Evaluate!", pages 130-132. Use the following suggestions to highlight important points and reinforce content.

- You may want to have students role-play the scenario.
- Direct students' attention to the "MediaWise" sidenote on page 130. Ask students to discuss why Americans spend more on video games than on movies.
- Direct students' attention to the "MediaWise" sidenote on page 131. Have students discuss their opinions of ratings for video games. Ask if video games should be rated? Why or why not?
- Have students read the questionnaire and discuss anything that is unclear. Then have students complete the questionnaire.
- Direct students' attention to the "MediaWise" sidenote on page 131. Ask questions such as these:
  - When have you used intuition? What was the result?
  - How would intuition be helpful in playing some video games?
- Direct students' attention to the "MediaWise" sidenote on page 132. Ask students to describe spin-offs they have seen or used.

Answers to Questionnaire

Students' answers will vary depending on the specific games they play and on their experience with those games. Obviously, there are no right or wrong answers. Instead, the questionnaire helps students explore the way they use video games. Emphasize that the questions present criteria or standards by which students can evaluate games and their use of those games. Encourage students to share their answers to the questionnaire. You may want to have students summarize the results.

Lesson 2

A DISKFULL OF KNOWLEDGE (PAGES 133-134)

Objective: Students evaluate CD-ROMS as sources of information.

Getting Started

Remind students that CD-ROMs are multimedia products. They combine audio and visual components in one product. Explain that we get 80 percent of our knowledge through our eyes, but we remember only 11 percent of it. We get a smaller percentage of knowledge through our ears, but remember more of it. By combining auditory and visual features, multimedia products can increase what we remember to 50 percent.

As further background, explain that 30 percent of all home computers sold in the United States in 1994 have CD-ROM drives. There are more than 10 million computer users in the United States who have CD-ROMs. Between 1993 and 1994, sales of CD-ROM disks increased from 7.6 million to 22.8 million.

Teaching Suggestions

Have students read "Lesson 2: A Diskful of Knowledge" (pages 133-134). Use the following suggestions to highlight important points and reinforce content.

- Draw students' attention to the "MediaWise" sidenote on page 133. You may want to have students thumb through a classroom reference book or textbook to get an idea of the number of pages of information a CD-ROM can hold. Explain that a new generation of CD-ROMs will be available in the late 1990s that can contain two or three times as much data.

- Make sure students are familiar with the print forms of the different reference works so that they can recognize some of the advantages and disadvantages of the multimedia formats. Ask questions such as the following:
  - For what purposes would you use an encyclopedia?
  - For what purposes would you use a dictionary?
  - For what purposes would you use an atlas?
  - For what purposes would you use an almanac?

- Discuss the list of pros and cons for information CD-ROMs. Explain that students may not have access to computers and information CD-ROMs and that knowing how to use the print forms is a valuable skill.

- Review the use of newspapers and magazines (Part 1) as sources of information. You may want to add to the list of topics, or have students add topics and discuss the appropriateness of print or multimedia resources for each topic.

Responses to Topics

Responses may vary depending on students' understanding of the topic and of print and multimedia references. Use the following guidelines to evaluate responses.

- For the mythical creature called a unicorn, students may choose either a print or multimedia encyclopedia. Students should recognize that they would get more information from a print source and that there would be limited advantage to having an audio feature for this topic, except for narration.

- For the history of the guitar, students should recognize that the audio feature of an informational CD-ROM would allow them to hear what a guitar sounds like as well as research music written for guitar throughout history. Some students may consider this an advantage over print information.

- For the biography of Maya Angelou, some students may choose CD-ROM as the resource because they might be able to hear the writer reading some of her works or they might hear the writer being interviewed. Other students may choose print resources because they would get more details about the writer's life.

- For a current problem in Buenos Aires, students should choose a print resource such as a newspaper or magazine. Students should recognize that information on CD-ROM is limited to the time the CD is made.

- For the "Discussion" on page 134, tell students to support their opinions with specific reasons. Encourage students to listen carefully to viewpoints that differ from their own.

Lesson 3

MY TEACHER: THE COMPUTER AND THE CD–ROM (PAGES 135-136)

Objective: Students compare and contrast computers with conventional methods of learning.

Getting Started

Have students discuss something they've learned recently and how they learned it. Topics might include mathematical skills, historical facts, science concepts, and physical skills such as dancing, ice skating, and slam dunking. Explain that we have many different ways of learning things.

Introduce the term *virtual reality*. Explain that this is a capability of computer software for creating situations that seem real. As an example, mention that virtual reality software has been used to cure people of the fear of high places. The computer creates a picture of what someone might see from a mountaintop or tall building. The picture is electronically sent to someone wearing a virtual-reality helmet and goggles. The person sees the "high" image, but is really standing on the ground. At first the person is scared. He or she thinks the picture is real. But slowly, the person gets used to the picture and the fear goes.

Ask students if they know of other examples of virtual-reality software. Have students discuss other possible uses based on the example given.

Teaching Suggestions

Have students read "Lesson 3: My Teacher: the Computer and the CD-ROM". Use the following suggestions to highlight important points and reinforce content.

- Ask if anyone has learned something by using a computer. Have volunteers describe their experience. Ask questions such as the following:
  - What did you learn?
  - What features of the computer hardware helped you?
  - What features of the computer software helped you?
  - Could you have learned the same thing another way? If so, how? If not, why not?
- Ask students to compare the computer and CD-ROM to a real teacher.
- Draw students' attention to the "MediaWise" sidenote on page 135. Students should anticipate that the number of computers in classrooms will increase in the future, because of the importance of computers in everyday life and the increasing applications for computers in education.
- Discuss the benefits of educational software. Ask students if any of these benefits surprise them, and, if so, why. Ask students what some of the disadvantages of educational software might be.
- Draw students' attention to the "MediaWise" sidenote on page 136. You may want to explain correspondence courses, which many people use to learn skills and earn college credits. Explain that the Virtual College is an electronic version that brings the classroom into the students' homes. Help students recognize that though some younger people might benefit from Virtual Middle School (such as some disabled children), bringing students together in a school or classroom has valuable social benefits that would be lost if students studied in isolation at home.

Responses to Subjects

Responses may vary according to students' understanding of the topic. Explain that deciding factors include how many minutes long or how thorough the educational software is, and the quality of the print materials available.

- For the human brain, students should agree that educational software would be a good choice. The software could provide diagrams, animation, and different points of view, as well as text and narration that would provide excellent information. On the other hand, some students may disagree, saying they would be able to obtain more detail from a book, which is probably true. The difference is that the software would present the information using more visual images.
- For swimming, students should conclude that software would not be a good choice because swimming is a physical sport that is best taught by someone who knows how to do it. It is also best taught in a swimming pool, an unlikely spot for a computer.
- For the history of Vietnam, some students may say software could provide valuable information through sound and pictures. Other students may say that print would give more facts and details.
- For Your Opinion, students should choose appropriate subjects and mention features of educational software that would enhance their learning (such as animation, graphics, and sound).

Unit Activity
YOUR CD-ROM WISH LIST
(PAGE 137)

- In this activity, students create lists of CD-ROMs they would like to have. You may choose to have students work independently or in small groups. Advise students to use the categories of CD-ROMs they have explored in this unit: games, informational, and educational.
- Follow up the activity by having groups summarize their wishes. What conclusions about CD-ROMS can the class as a whole draw?

Unit Evaluation
(PAGE 138)

Possible responses to the questions follow.

Checking What You Learned:

1. Students should check the first statement, "Video games are a major form of entertainment in America." Students should cite the fact that teens spend $6 billion on games and that companies like Broderbund earn tens of millions of dollars through sales of computer games.
2. Students may say that a CD-ROM encyclopedia is less expensive than a print encyclopedia, has multimedia, takes up a small amount of space, and is easy to use.
3. Students may cite advantages of multimedia, including sound and pictures; they may cite interactivity that allows them to go at their own pace. Students may cite drawbacks of CD-ROMs for teaching some skills that are better taught by humans, such as athletic skills.
4. Students should be able to cite some of the advantages of computers and CD-ROMs, such as multimedia and interactivity; they should be able to cite disadvantages, such as limited text and cost. Opinions may vary, but most students will probably conclude that computer hardware and software do have value.

Checking How You Learned:

Have students share and compare their answers. Encourage students to support their ideas with facts and examples.

UNIT 2

THE NET AND THE WEB
(PAGES 139-148)

Getting Started

Explain that this unit deals with the Internet and the World Wide Web. Write the word *Internet* on the board, pointing out that it is made up of a prefix, *inter* which means "between", "among", or "within", and *net* which stands for network, an interconnected system. Explain that *Internet* therefore means "connections among networks". Point out that the Internet is often referred to simply as "the Net". The Internet is actually a network of networks. Ask students how this kind of system might be useful to people.

If possible, arrange to have a computer with on-line capabilities available to the class. You may want to take students to the school media center or to the local library to demonstrate on-line features.

Teaching Suggestions

Have students read "Unit 2, "The Net and the Web", pages 139-146. Use the following suggestions to highlight important points and reinforce content.

What Is the Internet?

- Review the meaning of *network* and write the new term *hub* on the board. Draw students' attention to the illustration on page 139 and to the context of the word *hub*. Ask students to define hub using the illustration and context.

- Direct students' attention to the sidenote on page 139. Explain that as of 1995, North America had about 19 million Internet users. Europe had about 6,400,000. Asia had 920,000, and Central and South America had about 107,000. Many leaders in government, business, and education believe the Internet is part of a new "information revolution".

What Do You Need to Get Onto the Net?

- You may want to list the items on the board and discuss each one. The prices given are average as of 1995. Note that software for connecting to the Internet is usually included as part of the on-line hook-up fee, unlike other kinds of software such as CD-ROMs, which are expensive and sold separately.

- If students have not already done so in the Cooperative Learning activity on page 137, encourage them to explore possibilities for access to computers within their school and community. You may suggest that students prepare a list of available computers (and their capabilities).

How Do You Connect to the Internet?

- Explain that *electronic mail* is a system in which one person can type a message on a computer and send it to another person at a computer almost anywhere in the world. Both parties must be connected to an on-line system or to the Internet. The e-mail is sent over telephone wires or by satellite and reaches the other party in a second. Mention that some e-mail users refer to regular mail as "snail mail" because it is relatively much slower.

- Draw students' attention to the sidenote on page 140. You may want to have students find out which of the services is currently the most popular. In the fall of 1995, America On-Line was the leader with about 3 million subscribers.

- Write the terms *menu* and *download* on the board. Have students define the words using the context in which the words appear.

Lesson 1

USING THE NET
(PAGES 141-142)

Objective: Students make inferences about ways to use the Internet.

Getting Started

Ask students who have used the Internet to describe the features they used. If a computer is available, have students demonstrate how to access some Internet features. Alternatively, you may want to invite a computer-experienced person to visit the class and provide demonstrations. Explain that the Internet is a door to many, many sources of information and entertainment, but the Internet is not an end in itself; it is merely a tool. Explain that students need to recognize how the Internet can be used to help them pursue their interests and goals.

Teaching Suggestions

Have students read "Lesson 1: Using the Net", pages 141-142. Use the following suggestions to highlight important points and reinforce content.

- Ask students to discuss the advantages and disadvantages of e-mail, comparing it to other forms of communication, such as regular mail and telephone.
- Mention that in the mid 1990s web sites have become the hottest hang-out places for young people with computers. With cutting-edge graphics and the latest "buzz" on a multitude of topics, these sites attract millions of visitors each day. The popularity of a site is measured in the number of "hits" or visits by individuals. One site that was set up to advertise a movie received a million hits a day.
- Draw students' attention to the sidenote on page 142 regarding credit card information. Companies are making strides in securing this information so that users will feel that they can safely order products over the Internet. A degree of caution is still advisable, however.

Responses to How Would You Use the Internet?

Responses will vary depending on local conditions and students' interests and experience. Use the following suggestions to evaluate students' responses.

1. Students may cite the school computer lab, local library, or a local business if they do not have access to a computer at home.
2. Most students will probably select the World Wide Web because it offers the widest possibilities for information and entertainment. Some students may also choose Usenet groups or electronic mail.
3. Regardless of the subjects students choose, they should recognize that the World Wide Web and Usenet Groups would help them.
4. Students may mention using the Internet to get help with their homework, to communicate with pen pals or "key pals", to learn about job possibilities, to help their families plan vacations, and so on. The possibilities are endless.

Lesson 3

EVALUATING WHAT YOU GET FROM THE NET (PAGES 143-144)

Objective: Students evaluate the Internet as a source of information.

Getting Started

Ask students to recall methods they learned for analyzing and evaluating sources of information in Part 2 ("Focus on Audio Media"), Unit 1, Lesson 1 (pages 42-44) and Lesson 2 (pages 45-47). Students should recall questions such as these: What supporting evidence is there? Is the evidence valid? Is it good? Why is it good? How well does it do what it is supposed to do? Does the information make sense? Is the information accurate? Is the information from a good or reliable source? Are the opinions fair and balanced? Do other sources agree with this one? Explain that students can apply the same questions to information they get on the Internet.

Teaching Suggestions

Have students read "Lesson 2: Evaluating What You Get From the Net", pages 143-144. Use the following suggestions to highlight important points and reinforce content.

- Emphasize that the Internet is so vast and involves so many people that it is a user-beware situation. This is especially true regarding information. There is no central monitor or standard by which information is evaluated before it is put on-line.
- Draw students' attention to the sidenote on page 143 regarding anonymity. In a brochure titled "Child Safety on the Information Highway" (available free from the National Center for Missing and Exploited Children at 1-800-THE-LOST), Lawrence J. Magid suggests six safety rules for young Internet users: 1. not giving out personal information without your parents' permission; 2. telling parents if you find information that makes you feel uncomfortable; 3. never agreeing to meet with someone in person whom you've contacted on-line, except with your parents' permission; 4. never sending a picture to anyone without your parents' approval; 5. not sending mean messages to anyone; 6. setting up rules of Internet use with your parents.
- Discuss the guidelines for evaluating information. Also suggest that students double-check Internet information by consulting a print resource.

Answers to Questions on Pages 144

1. Students should recognize that TJLore's opinion is biased because the skater lives in Hoboken. TJLore may never have skated anywhere else, so the opinion is not reliable.

2. Students should recognize that they could check another Web site related to skating, call a skating association, or read a skating magazine.

3. Students should recognize Skylar's credentials: running a sports rink and belonging to a skating association. Skylar also makes a useful recommendation for getting more information.

4. Students might suggest topics such as recreation, in-line skating, skating, athletics, hobbies, and sports.

5. Answers will vary. A simple experience is looking a word up in a dictionary and then looking the word up in a another dictionary or in an encyclopedia. In trying to locate a place (in the supermarket, in a city, and so on) students may have asked several people until they got the right directions.

Lesson 3

INTERVIEW WITH A NET USER (PAGES 145-146)

Objective: Students will compare ideas about using the Internet with the experiences of an actual Internet user.

Getting Started

If you have not had an opportunity to invite a computer-user (specifically an Internet user) to visit the class, consider doing so for this lesson. You might ask another teacher, a librarian, or a student in a higher grade level. Alternatively, it may be the case that most students will know someone who uses the Internet whom they can interview.

Teaching Suggestions

Have students read "Lesson 3: Interview With a Net User", pages 145-146. Use the following suggestions to highlight important points and reinforce content.

- Have students identify candidates for their

interview. Students should also describe how they intend to interview the Net users. You may want to have students brainstorm questions to ask the Net users.

Responses to Interview

Students' interviews will vary, but you should look for specific responses to each of the five questions suggested on page 145. Encourage students to share the results of their interviews.

- For the "Discussion" on page 146, tell students to support their opinions with specific reasons. Encourage students to listen carefully to viewpoints that differ from their own.

Unit Activity
YOUR ROAD MAP TO GETTING ON THE INTERNET (PAGE 147)

- In this cooperative learning activity, students will use the guidelines provided to access and obtain information from the Internet. Before students begin the activity, you may want to arrange time for students to use computers in the school library or school computer center. You should also arrange to have an experienced Internet user available (such as the librarian or an advanced student) to assist students. Encourage students to brainstorm topics they would like to explore on the Internet. Point out that procedures for accessing the Internet may vary somewhat, depending on the on-line service used. You can find additional tips and guidelines for accessing the Internet in books such as *Kids On-Line* by Marian Salzman and Robert Pondiscio (Avon Books, 1959), and *The Whole Internet* by Ed Kroll (O'Reilley & Associates, 1994).

- Follow up the activity by having groups compare their experiences. What conclusions about using the Internet can the class as a whole draw?

Unit Evaluation
(PAGE 148)

Possible responses to the questions follow.

Checking What You Learned:

1. Students should choose "c", explaining that the Internet is made up of thousands of computers linked in groups or networks called hubs. These networks are linked to each other, so that the Net is really a network of networks.
2. Students should mark the first and third statements. They should explain that access to the Internet can be costly because it requires costly equipment, including a computer, modem, and telephone time. Students should explain that access to computers is possible through local libraries, school computer centers, local businesses, and other community resources.
3. Students should cite these strategies: deciding whether information is fact or opinion; considering the source of the information and evidence that the information is accurate; and checking additional sources of information.
4. Answers may vary, but students should recognize that the Internet provides many sources of information that students can use in various ways, from hobbies to homework.

Checking How You Learned:

Have students share and compare their answers. Encourage students to support their ideas with facts and examples.

ADVERTISING ON LINE
(PAGES 149-150)

Getting Started

Have students describe how they might use the Internet to advertise a product. Review some of the features of on-line communication, such as graphics, sound, interactivity, and a worldwide audience. Ask students how advertisers might use these features.

Teaching Suggestions

Have students read the feature on advertising on-line, pages 149-150. You may want to direct students to stop occasionally to allow for class discussion. Use the following suggestions to highlight important points and reinforce content.

- A survey in the fall of 1995 found that 67 percent of those who use the Internet are male. Over half of these users are between 18 and 34 years of age. The median household income for these people was $50,000 to $75,000.

- Among the biggest advertisers on-line are movie studios, offering stills, cast biographies, soundtracks, press kits, interactive games, storyboards, and trailers that can be downloaded. Visitors can send e-mail to actors and directors.

- Even though Internet users do not tune into the same web pages at once, the way they would tune into a TV show, a single web site can still receive millions of "hits" or visits over a period of time. In the summer of 1995, Time Warner's "Batman Forever" home page received 1.8 million hits a week.

Answers to Questions on Page 150

1. Students should cite the fact that advertisers have no way of presenting themselves to Internet users except at the users' choice. In addition, Internet users can click off to another web site if they find an advertisement boring or uninteresting.

2. Among advantages students should cite are the ability to provide sound, games, and even motion pictures on-line. On-line users can also make purchase's directly on-line by inputting credit card information.

- For the Activity on page 150, suggest that student groups share their final plans.

PROJECT
CREATING A WEB PAGE
(PAGES 151-154)

- Lead into the project by asking students to describe any web pages they have seen and used. Guide students in listing some of the possible features of a web page, aside from the page's specific topic. These features include sound, graphics, words, and hypertext.

- The following questions may help you evaluate students' performance on the project: Were students able to work together to identify an appropriate topic for their page? Did students describe ways to utilize web site capabilities? Were students' ideas expressed clearly? Were students able to explain their pages and provide useful feedback to other groups?

BIBLIOGRAPHY

ABOUT THE REPRODUCIBLE MASTERS

The four "Getting the Message" reproducible masters comprise a culminating project that will help students consider what they have learned in *Media Today*. Divide the class into three groups. Give Sheet 1 to each member of Group 1; give Sheets 2 and 3 to members of the corresponding groups. Be sure students in Groups 1 and 3 are prepared either to take notes or to record their programs as specified on their sheets. After groups have made their presentations to the class, distribute Sheet 4 to each student to complete.

Two additional reproducible masters, "Preparing for a Debate" and "Self-Evaluation Form for Group Activities", are also provided for student use.

FOR ADDITIONAL REFERENCE

Items marked with an asterisk are suitable for students as well as teachers.

PART 1: NEWSPAPERS AND MAGAZINES

Click, J.W., and Russel Baird. *Magazine Editing and Production.* Dubuque, IA: W.C. Brown, 1986.

Folio: *The Magazine for Magazine Management.* Any issue.

Rothmyer, Karen. *Winning Pulitzers: The Stories Behind Some of the Best Coverage of Our Time.* New York: Columbia University Press, 1991.

Scholastic Update. May 7, 1993 (advertising special issue).

PART 2: AUDIO MEDIA

*DeCurtis, Anthony, and James Henke. *The Rolling Stone Illustrated History of Rock and Roll.* New York: Random House, 1992.

Sterling, Christopher, and John Kittross. *Stay Tuned: A Concise History of Broadcasting in the United States.* Belmont, CA: Wadsworth, 1990.

PART 3: TELEVISION AND MOVIES

*Carnes, Mark C. *Past Imperfect: History According to the Movies.* New York: Henry Holt & Co., 1995.

Entertainment Weekly. Any issue. (Besides articles on TV and films, this magazine also regularly reviews CD-ROMs, books, and recordings.)

Goodwin, Andrew. *Dancing in the Distraction Factory: Music Television and Popular Culture.* Minneapolis: University of Minnesota Press, 1992.

*Robertson, Patrick. *The Guinness Book of Movie Facts and Feats.* New York: Abbeville Press Publishers, 1994.

*Winn, Marie. *The Plug-In Drug.* New York: Viking Penguin, 1985.

Winship, Michael. *Television.* New York: Random House, 1988. (This is the companion book to the PBS television series.)

PART 4: COMPUTER-BASED MEDIA

*Godin, Seth. *Best of the Net: The Most Useful, Fascinating, and (Occasionally) Weird Stuff on the Internet.* San Mateo, CA: IDG Books Worldwide, 1995.

Hoffman, Paul. *The Internet.* San Mateo, CA: IDG Books Worldwide, 1995.

Kent, Peter. *The Complete Idiot's Guide to the World Wide Web.* Indianapolis: Alpha Books, 1995.

*Rimmer, Steve. *Planet Internet.* New York: McGraw-Hill, 1995.

*Salzman, Miriam, and Robert Pondiscio. *Kids On-Line.* New York: Avon Books, 1995.

1. TELEVISION

Name: _____ **Date:** _____

GETTING THE MESSAGE
"Getting the Message" sheets 1-4 will help you evaluate your media literacy.

Starting Up
Form a small group. Each group member should watch a different kind of TV program. Here are some examples:

sitcom   *drama*   *infomercial*   *news magazine*

Either videotape the shows or take notes about them to share with the class.

Planning
Work with your group to choose two of the shows. Study these shows together. Answer the following questions about each one.

1. Is the show's main purpose to entertain, to inform, or to persuade? Does it have more than one purpose?

_____

2. Who is the show's target audience?

_____

3. What clues make you think that this is the target audience?

_____

4. What techniques does the show use to reach and hold its audience?

_____

5. In what ways might watching this show shape your views?

_____

Write a plan of what group members will say to present your ideas to the class.

Presenting Your Analysis
Share the show and your analysis with the class.

2. PRINT MEDIA

Name: _____   **Date:** _____

GETTING THE MESSAGE

"Getting the Message" sheets 1-4 will help you evaluate your media literacy.

Starting Up

Form a small group. Choose one magazine or newspaper. Each group member should read different articles or features.

Bring in the newspaper or magazine or photocopy sections to share with the class.

Planning

Work with your group. Study the magazine or newspaper you have chosen. Answer the following questions.

1. Is its main purpose to entertain, to inform, or to persuade? Does it have more than one purpose?

_____

2. Who is its target audience?

_____

3. What clues make you think that this is the target audience?

_____

4. What techniques does the magazine or newspaper use to reach and hold its audience?

_____

5. In what ways might reading this newspaper or magazine shape your views?

_____

Write a plan of what group members will say to present your ideas to the class.

Presenting Your Analysis

Share the newspaper or magazine and your analysis with the class.

3. RADIO

Name: **Date:**

GETTING THE MESSAGE
"Getting the Message" sheets 1-4 will help you evaluate your media literacy.

Starting Up
Form a small group. Each group member should listen to a different kind of radio program. At least one program should be a news or informational program.

Either tape-record the shows or take notes about them to share with the class.

Planning
Work with your group. Study two of the programs you have chosen. Answer the following questions about each one.

1. Is its main purpose to entertain, to inform, or to persuade? Does it have more than one purpose?

_____

2. Who is its target audience?

_____

3. What clues make you think that this is the target audience?

_____

4. What techniques does the program use to reach and hold its audience?

_____

5. In what ways might listening to this program shape your views?

_____

Write a plan of what group members will say to present your ideas to the class.

Presenting Your Analysis
Share the radio programs and your analysis with the class.

4. BE MEDIA WISE

Name: **Date:**

GETTING THE MESSAGE

"Getting the Message" sheets 1-4 will help you evaluate your media literacy.

Work with the class. Compare your findings on TV, print media, and radio. Then complete the sections below.

How the forms of media are alike:

_____

_____

How the forms of media are different:

_____

_____

What conclusions can you draw about how different media get their messages across?

_____

_____

List your tips for becoming a media-wise reader.

- _____
- _____
- _____

List your tips for becoming a media-wise listener.

- _____
- _____
- _____

List your tips for becoming a media-wise viewer.

- _____
- _____
- _____

DEBATE

Name: _____   **Date:** _____

PREPARING FOR A DEBATE

Wise debaters plan their arguments in advance. To plan effectively, consider what arguments the other side may use. Complete this sheet to help you plan.

The question or issue to be debated:

_____

_____

My position:

_____

_____

Arguments in support of my position:

_____

_____

Arguments the other side may use against my position:

_____

_____

Make a debating plan. List your main points in a logical order. After each point, write facts, reasons, and examples to support it.

Main point: _____

Support: _____

Main point: _____

Support: _____

Main point: _____

Support: _____

Main point: _____

Support: _____

Name: **Date:**

SELF-EVALAUTION FORM FOR GROUP ACTIVITIES

Use the following questions to evaluate your contribution to a group activity or project.

1. What was the group activity or project in which you participated?

_____

2. What were your responsibilities in the group?

_____

3. What contributions did you make to the group?

_____

4. Did you help other group members? How?

_____

5. On a scale of 1 to 10 (10 being the highest), how would you rate your contribution to the group? Explain your reasons.

_____

6. How could you have contributed more?

_____

7. Did the group use time well? Why or why not?

_____

8. Overall, how well did the group work together? How could the group have worked more effectively?

_____

9. What have you learned from the experience?

_____

Teach your students to think critically about the media!

MEDIA TODAY

Interpreting Newspapers, Magazines, Radio, TV, Movies and the Internet

Now you can provide your students with relevant applications of critical thinking skills by analyzing the media.

Everyday, Americans of all ages are bombarded by enormous quantities of information at an extraordinarily fast pace. *Media Today* prepares your students for success in the information age by developing essential skills for media literacy.

This innovative book helps your students to successfully comprehend, analyze, synthesize, and evaluate the ideas and information they receive from the media. The program covers the four main media categories:

Print • Radio • Television/Movies • Multimedia/Internet.

Students come to understand the media that is so powerful in our society.

Media Today draws on high-interest topics to teach essential skills in reading, listening, viewing, and thinking.

Topics include:

Talk Show Hosts

Advertising

Inflammatory Radio

Pop Music

The World Wide Web

Call 1-800-848-9500 for information or customer service.
ISBN: 0-8359-1924-2

Globe Fearon Educational Publisher
A Division of Simon & Schuster
Upper Saddle River, New Jersey

ISBN 0-8359-192...

9 780835 919241